Mozart

Mozart

HENRY RAYNOR

M

To E:

Copyright © Henry Raynor 1978

All rights reserved. No part of this publication may be reproduced or transmitted, in any form or by any means, without permission.

First published 1978 by
MACMILLAN LONDON LIMITED
London and Basingstoke

Associated companies in Delhi, Dublin, Hong Kong, Johannesburg, Lagos, Melbourne, New York, Singapore and Tokyo

Printed in Hong Kong

British Library Cataloguing in Publication Data
Raynor, Henry
    Mozart.
    1. Mozart, Wolfgang Amadeus
    2. Composers, Austrian—Biography
    780'.92'4   ML410.M9
    ISBN 0-333-21615-6

Contents

Introduction

Wolfgang Amadeus Mozart composed music because to do so was both his nature and his profession. His was perhaps the finest creative mind to express itself through music because he reached a state in which he could allow his music to convey its own nature, untrammelled by personal emotions and experiences.

It is in some ways appropriate that the most magnificently gifted of musicians should in worldly terms have been a failure apparently born to tragedy. Mozart's life was tragic not in the loose modern sense which applies the term to any sad chapter of accidents: his was the classical tragedy, which ancient Greeks would have understood, of a man of great gifts and unusual strength destroyed by the single flaw in his character. Feckless, extravagant, lazy, unwilling to face hostile facts, Mozart's weaknesses grew from his certainty of his own superior gifts: because he was

Mozart, and demonstrably great, the world would not let him perish. Even at the end, defeated, despairing and believing himself poisoned, his music continued to transcend his own experience and his downfall.

Each succeeding age has found the qualities it needed to find in the work of Mozart, but of all periods it is perhaps our own which gains most from the music he left, ranging as it does across everyday experience to great emotional intensities and spiritual exaltations, rejecting nothing in life except the slipshod, the clumsy and the incompletely realised.

That, it may be, is why in our uncertain, disorganised, formless age, when the clumsily unrealised is greeted as the eruption of genius and when standards of emotional and intellectual integrity seem to be out of reach, Mozart's music is at its most popular.

1 Salzburg and the Mozarts

In 1737 Leopold Mozart, the eighteen-year-old son of an Augsburg bookbinder, arrived in Salzburg. He had been a choirboy and a gifted young organist in his native city, and the church authorities there had guided him to Salzburg University as a theology student. He was a small, handsome young man, serious minded, a devout Catholic of such rigidly high principles that his patrons must have been surprised and disappointed that he enrolled at the university as a student of law; he had ambitions and interests beyond those of the son of the average artisan, and the priesthood, it seems, was not the way to satisfy them.

Naturally the Augsburg church authorities cast him off, and he financed his studies by working as *valet de chambre* to the President of the Salzburg cathedral chapter, the equivalent of the dean of an English cathedral. The post was less servile than its equivalent would be today; a *valet de chambre* was necessarily a man of some education, for as well as the duties we consider appropriate to those of a valet he acted as his master's personal private secretary. Leopold, having cheated his original patrons to get his feet on the lower rungs of the ladder, began to establish himself as a musician. He composed a set of rather old-fashioned trio sonatas, harking back to the style of the baroque composers, and dedicated them to his master. He provided incidental music for a Latin play produced at the university; he wrote whatever music would come in useful at court, at the cathedral and for the domestic music-making of friends. In 1743 he became violin teacher at the cathedral choir school and was appointed one of the Archbishop's court composers; this was an appointment which meant that he was rarely expected to supply specific works on demand but

that when music was needed from him he should supply it, and that anything he composed might be taken over for use in court. His employer was not only a considerable ecclesiastical authority; by birth he was Count Thurn und Taxis, a member of a family which exercised great political and social authority. Leopold composed an oratorio, *Christ's Burial*, for Lent. He became a violinist in the Archbishop's orchestra and found that he had a certain facility for composing amusing entertainment music often scored for eccentric instruments: his 'Hunting' Symphony, for example, is for strings, horns and, in the trio, dogs and rifle. He composed the 'Toy' Symphony which uses toy instruments and was for many years attributed to Joseph Haydn. A cautious, thoughtful man, determined to preserve his security, by 1747 he felt confident enough to marry Anna Maria Pertl of St Gilgen; her family owned a little land and her father was warden of a charity home.

Leopold and Anna Maria produced their first-born son, Johann Joachim, in 1748, but he died in 1749; a daughter born in June 1749 lived for a week; a third child, another girl, survived for eleven weeks. The next child, Maria Anna Walburga (known in the family as 'Nannerl'), was born in July 1751 and lived to a ripe old age; she was famous in her childhood, lapsing into an apparently contented obscurity in her adolescence. A further short-lived son and daughter were born in 1752 and 1754, but in 1756 the seventh child, Johann Chrysostom Wolfgang Amadeus, survived. He owed the name Johann Chrysostom to his birth on that saint's day. Eighteenth-century infant mortality rates are, at their best, shocking, but the production of five babies incapable of surviving suggests that there might have been some other reason, still unknown, than

*Leopold Mozart, c. 1762. A pencil drawing by Franz
Lactanz.*

9

eighteenth-century ignorance for the survival of only two out of seven children, particularly as these two seemed to be an easy target for any disease available in Europe.

By the time Wolfgang was born Leopold, approaching the age of thirty-seven, had climbed the ladder of Salzburg music almost as high as he was to reach. The composer–critic Friedrich Wilhelm Marpurg reviewed Leopold's most famous work, the textbook *Versuch einer gründlichen Violinschule*, with lavish praise in 1757, and a report on Salzburg music in the same yearbook, Marpurg's *Historisch-kritische Beiträge zur Aufnahme der Musik*, claims that a good deal of Leopold's work was known in manuscript: Marpurg referred to numerous contrapuntal church pieces, twelve oratorios, a large number of symphonies, orchestral serenades, chamber music and occasional pieces like the 'Musical Sleigh-Ride', noting Leopold's cleverness with unorthodox instruments. Leopold, in other words, was a typical court musician, inclined in his serious music to be

The University Church and college buildings in Salzburg in 1735.

rather stodgy though invariably correct, but with an unexpected gift for amusing entertainment music. His *Violin School* remained the best authority on violin technique until Paganini's tours in the 1820s and 1830s introduced an enormous range of new techniques and effects.

The musical establishment at Salzburg was quite imposing. The Archbishop's orchestra, in the year of Wolfgang's birth, had thirty-six players, supplemented whenever necessary by the town musicians and the trumpets and drums of the Archbishop's militia. In addition, the choir and soloists of the cathedral were available for performances in court. The town had its theatre to which touring companies brought plays and operas, though court opera in Salzburg was mounted only to celebrate some special event and was given in the *Karabinierisaal* of the Residenz.

Salzburg had been an ecclesiastical state, its Archbishop being its Prince, since 1281. The city as we know it and as the Mozarts knew it was the legacy of the greatest of the Prince Archbishops, Wolf Dietrich, enthroned in 1587. Bavarian on his father's side, his mother was a Medici, and Wolf Dietrich inherited the tastes and ideas of his Italian relations. During his reign he rebuilt Salzburg Cathedral and the Residenz, creating the Mirabel Palace to be a home for his mistress and their children: he turned medieval Salzburg into the splendid baroque city which we know.

Wolf Dietrich's toleration of Protestantism annoyed both the Pope and the Emperor, and his almost matrimonial way of life provided an excuse for his enemies. The Dukes of Bavaria revived an old claim to Salzburg and its territories. Neither the Pope nor the Emperor could countenance the Bavarian claim, and they joined forces to drive the Bavarian invaders out of the little principality and remove Wolf Dietrich, who was exiled and imprisoned. His successors followed his policies, extending both the beautiful baroque city and Wolf Dietrich's Italianate taste in music.

In 1737, the year in which Leopold Mozart began his studies at Salzburg University, J. G. Eberlin was appointed *Kapellmeister*. Before that he had been fourth organist. The vice-*Kapellmeister* appointed at the time of Eberlin's promotion was Francesco Giuseppe Lolli, who had arrived in the principality with Eberlin. The two were little older than Leopold and, though Leopold seemed unable at first to accept the fact, blocked his way to further promotion. In 1742 Anton Cajetan Adlgasser became court cembalist, and in 1762 Michael Haydn, the younger and at that time more highly regarded brother of the great Joseph, became organist at St Peter's monastery church and a court composer. In 1762 Eberlin died and Leopold achieved his promotion to vice-*Kapellmeister*.

Apart from these musical changes in the *dramatis personae*, a new Prince Archbishop had been enthroned in 1753. Sigismund Christoph von

Mozart's birthplace in the Löchelplatz (No. 225 is marked).

Above: The new baroque Salzburg Cathedral was rebuilt by the greatest of the Prince Archbishops, Wolf Dietrich.

Right: Archbishop Sigismund Christoph von Schrattenbach, who was enthroned in 1753.

Schrattenbach was fundamentally an easy-going man. With an efficient though pedestrian musical staff there was no reason to disturb the senior authorities in the *Kapell* simply to replace the pedestrian Lolli with the equally pedestrian Leopold Mozart. Schrattenbach helped Leopold by accepting the dedication of his *Violin School*, perhaps realising that whatever genius Leopold showed was that of a teacher, not of a creative musician.

Leopold was an upright man with a hard practical sense of the possible and how it could be attained. In Salzburg he was always conscious of being worth more than he was allowed to be. Musically however he was not the superior of his

12

Reverendissimus
et Celsissimus
Dominus Dominus
SIGISMUNDUS CHRISTOPHORUS
Archiepiscopus et S. R. I. Princeps
Salisburgensis, Sacræ Sedis Apostolicæ
Legatus Natus, Germaniæ Primas,
ex Illust.ma Prosapiâ Comitum
de Schrattenbach,
&c. &c.

fellow vice-*Kapellmeister*, and his sense of superiority overrode his realism. He was a graduate, an educated man, and in Catholic southern Europe it was rare for any musician to be more than a musician. Leopold took note of the world and its politics, was interested in painting, had a lively sense of architectural decency, and in this way was isolated from his colleagues. He was conscious that they were, in education and culture, his inferiors. Only one Salzburg musician, the court trumpeter Andreas Schachtner, became a close friend, and Schachtner, like Leopold, was an educated man. Not only was he a tolerable violinist and cellist as well as a trumpeter; when *Idomeneo* was produced at Munich, Schachtner wrote the translation of the libretto printed in the first programme, and when Wolfgang, at Salzburg, decided to try to draw attention with a German opera—the unfinished *Zaide*—Schachtner was his librettist, apparently working scene by scene with Wolfgang, for there are no words for more of the work than was composed before Mozart abandoned it.

Leopold's friends, apart from Schachtner, seem to have been members of the city's intelligentsia—the clergy of the middle rank, like Abbé Bullinger, the private chaplain of the court chamberlain Count Arco. It was his grocer–landlord, Lorenz Hagenauer, who was favoured with the letters which described the triumphs of the first concert tour across Germany to France and England.

For all Leopold's probity (for, having once displayed some talent for duplicity in order to reach university, he made no further use of it until his son was growing up) and intelligence, he was a member of a musical organisation some members of which he could not see as his musical superiors; their facility was greater, their pens readier, their flow of ideas more extensive or their versatility more marked. Schrattenbach was prepared to accept the dedication of Leopold's most successful work, but apart from such helpful courtesies he seems to have had little real interest in music. Some hundred singers and instrumentalists were under his control, and of them Leopold was one of the most senior. But Leopold, like all musicians except those who could turn out a regular supply of successful operas, was a poor man. His salary was 300 gulden a year, with a subsistence allowance of 54 gulden because he lived in the town and was not quartered with the musicians in court; a re-allotment of work in 1778 brought him a further 100 gulden.

Of course Salzburg, as a capital city, had as well as its court and government authorities a *bourgeoisie*, some of whom were wealthy enough to be potential patrons of the arts. Its theatre was a public institution, and there was an audience for concert music outside the court. Families like that of Count Andretter, the Minister for War, were prepared to commission music for family celebrations, and Andretter was responsible for Wolfgang's Serenade K. 185 for the marriage of his daughter in 1773; the musician was not completely restricted to his exiguous official pay. Greater than a mere minister was the middle-class Siegmund Haffner, an international banker who paid the Archbishop's treasury 26,000 gulden each year to have his ledgers exempt from official scrutiny; he kept on other interests in Salzburg because they were always profitable. Haffner was, among other things, a one-man building society, granting loans of mortgage with property as security. He also served as Burgomaster of Salzburg. It was natural for a man of such distinction and wealth to celebrate great family events in music; the marriage of his daughter drew from Wolfgang the splendid Serenade K. 250, and his ennoblement the serenade which eventually, losing a movement, became the 'Haffner' Symphony (K. 385).

Wolfgang Mozart was lucky in his father, a fine teacher who knew all the rules and gave him all the teaching he wanted. The society into which he was born was, however, far less to his advantage: the world of Salzburg music was pedestrian and workaday, satisfying only the less ambitious tastes and appetites.

2 The Wunderkind

Probably there never was a more gifted child than Wolfgang. Other musical children have shown marvellous gifts and have lived to develop them, and Mendelssohn at the age of thirteen or fourteen possibly had a more original mind than Mozart at the same age but did not as a man fulfil the promise of his youth. Where Mozart differed from other prodigies was in the lucidity and sense of proportion, the instinctive qualities of form and design, which are apparent in the earliest little works which his father wrote down at his dictation before he himself could write. When Leopold and Andreas Schachtner found the four-year-old boy with a sheet of writing paper liberally smeared with ink, he declared that he was writing a concerto. Leopold indulgently pushed the inky manuscript on one side; it was Schachtner who pointed out that the manuscript showed all the signs of a genuine attempt at composition. Leopold looked at the paper with amazement and told Wolfgang, who went to the piano to play what he had written, that the music was too hard to be played at all. 'It has to be hard because it's a concerto', the little boy had replied.

The elder child, Nannerl, was herself a remarkable keyboard player, stylish and precise. She does not seem to have been remarkable in any other way. Her diary is interesting in what it has to say about her brother, but it never succeeds in making us aware of her own personality. By the time Wolfgang was three, Nannerl was eight and receiving Leopold's obviously first-rate teaching. The lessons fascinated Wolfgang, who joined in them, finding interesting chords and being specially pleased by thirds and sixths. Though the boy never had a tolerable singing voice, at three he could remember not only melodies but harmonies and chord progressions, and he seems to have had a still rarer gift—an immediate sense of form, of the natural evolution of a melody to its own inevitable, fulfilling shape.

As Mozart's mind apparently even from these

Previous page: Mozart with a bird's nest, painted by Zoffany in London between 1764 and 1765.

early years worked at full power only in matters of music, it was music itself which inspired him to compose. When he heard new music which was, in his favourite term of approbation, 'effective', he based his own style upon it. He did not copy but rather mastered the style of whatever impressed him—a practice which continued all his life. Nothing but music seemed to stimulate his creative mind. When he began to add his contributions to the voluminous family correspondence, the crowded impressions which should have filled his head between his sixth and fourteenth years— the great German cities, Paris and Versailles and the Tuileries, the 'white cliffs of Dover' and the amazing muddle of London, where varieties of splendour and squalor were jumbled cheek by jowl—these things are never mentioned. The middle ages, as they survived in streets and buildings, he simply disliked: to him, Nuremberg was an ugly little town. It is Leopold who shows an interest in the visual arts and seems to have studied them with pleasure and intelligence. There is no indication that Wolfgang so much as noticed the glories of Italy during his first visit; so far as we can tell from the letters his attention was not caught, and he seems never to have looked at a picture, a carving or a building for his own pleasure. From the beginning, the arts to him were music and drama—those in which he was supreme, for Mozart's music was essentially dramatic and through music he understood the theatre. As a child, mathematics delighted him; his sister recalled how elementary arithmetic fascinated him so much that he covered the walls and furniture of the family apartment with chalk figures and sums. Naturally Leopold, a serious-minded man, was not content to bring up a musical genius who remained otherwise uneducated.

What Frau Mozart thought about her unusually gifted daughter and her amazing son we do not know. Anna Maria was not, it seems, a very healthy woman, but the Mozartian gaiety and lightness of spirit, qualities which Wolfgang never lost even in affliction, seem to have been inherited from her. Leopold, despite his gift for amusing entertainment music, was a rather solemn man whose seriousness of outlook could easily turn into disgruntled sourness; but he adored his son. The Mozart household could never have been rich, but it was close and devoted, willingly giving Wolfgang the affection for which he clamoured. The child needed to be loved and assured of love; to tease him by suggesting that he was not loved as dearly as he wished was to send him away in tears until convincing reassurance was provided.

The centre of Wolfgang's world was his father, who, he said and believed, came only a single step behind God in authority and power. To end each day, from the time when he could first do so until he was more than ten years old, the little boy earned his goodnight kiss by standing on a chair and singing a nonsense song in his father's honour to a tune that seems to have been evolved from the Dutch folk-song 'Wilhelmus van Nassouwe'. This quite early on seems to have become a duet, Leopold singing a bass to his son's treble. Its words, apparently, were nonsense made up by Wolfgang, already aware of the sound of Italian but too young to attach any meaning to its flowing, liquid syllables:

> Oragno figata fa,
> Marina gamina fa.

Much of the young Wolfgang's life seems to have been turned into ceremonies with their own music; he enjoyed the idea that moving from room to room, taking up or putting away a favourite toy, and the routine duties of his day should be activities with their proper musical accompaniments. His childish energy, so to speak, was linked to or harnessed by organised rhythms. He was an almost unnaturally good child, lively, sociable, high-spirited but always entirely amenable. To Leopold, the little boy seems to have been at first an entrancing toy, loving to be taught not only music but every subject that was put before him; learning was simply another game, and Leopold was a fine teacher. Only two things ever seem

to have disturbed Wolfgang: one was to be asked to play to listeners who treated music with less than proper reverence, and the other was the sound of an unaccompanied trumpet, which terrified him. Leopold, acting like any father determined to toughen up a boy suffering from a foolish weakness, startled him with trumpets played loudly to convince the child of their harmlessness.

Wolfgang's incredible musical progress was as miraculous to Leopold as it was to every adult who heard it. As soon as the boy was six, Leopold set out to show him to the world; oddly enough, Leopold did not display his marvellous son to his patron, Archbishop Schrattenbach, until the child had made a sensation elsewhere, although the Archbishop was more indulgent than many men

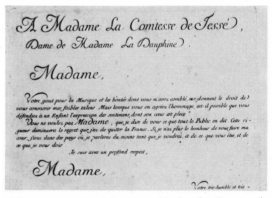

Mozart was only eight years old when his Sonatas for piano and violin, dedicated to La Comtesse de Tessé, were published in April 1764.

in his position would have been to servants who asked to be on leave more often than they were on duty, and apparently remained well-disposed to the Mozarts because they did not personally inconvenience him.

For the next nine years the Mozarts lived like gypsies, showing the world what Wolfgang and Nannerl could do. It was probably as a result of this that Wolfgang, who never lived to reach his thirty-sixth birthday, always gave an impression of physical frailty and that in spite of his uncertain finances he seemed to find it impossible to live in one place for any length of time. As a married man in Vienna he changed lodgings over and over again, apparently for no reason than a wish to be somewhere else. His childhood tours meant that he endured not only the tribulations of eighteenth-century travel but also the wear and tear on his nerves which is the lot of any performing artist. Quite possibly, for a six-year-old, playing to the

The six-year-old Mozart plays to Maria Theresa, Empress of Austria, and Marie Antoinette. A painting by E. Ender.

hard to believe that his performances continued without nervous strain. For the supersensitive boy at puberty, responding with intensity to people as well as to music, and the young adolescent living among professional musicians and working as a professional in a world of often bitter competition, there must have been times when the strains of travel, of performance and of competition were close to unbearable. Though nineteenth-century opinion attempted to make Mozart into a serene, untroubled angelic spirit, his contemporaries thought of him as a balanced, friendly person whom it was natural to love. Leopold's loving exploitation seems to have done him far less harm than might have been expected.

Three weeks in Vienna, when Wolfgang was six, launched him on the world as a *Wunderkind*. He and Nannerl played to the Empress Maria Theresa and the Austrian nobility. Their performances produced praise and presents, and Leopold was left with five months at home in Salzburg in which to plan his great international tour of Germany, France and London. If it is strange to the twentieth century that a devoted father should so put at risk the physical and mental health of a son whom he adored, he never realised, any more than did anyone in the eighteenth century, that children are not by nature simply small adults. Probably to Leopold the magical thing about his son was not that such a child should exist at all, but simply that so minute a human being could learn enough in a short time to beat most adults at their own game. Childhood as something different in nature from adulthood was the discovery of the early romantic movement, and Leopold was no romantic.

A good deal was written in letters and diaries about both the Mozart children; naturally, Wolfgang attracted more attention than Nannerl, and his admirers—and everyone he met was an admirer—write not only about his incredible gifts but also about his liveliness, his lovableness and his occasional delightful lapses into childishness. The Hon. Daines Barrington, who met the *Wun-*

Empress Maria Theresa (who made an almost maternal fuss of him) meant no more than playing to Anna Maria, Leopold and their friends at home on the Löchelplatz—an enjoyable way of spending time. But as the years passed and the child was submitted to tests of all sorts to try his musicianship, versatility, musicality and originality, it is

derkind in London in June 1765, prepared a report for the Royal Society (which was not delivered until 1769) describing the various tests he set for the boy; he noted that the coming of a cat into the room was sufficient distraction to an eight-year-old to prevent either Barrington or Leopold getting him back to the harpsichord for 'a considerable time', and that Wolfgang would at times turn away from music and 'run about the room with a stick between his legs by way of a horse'. None of these eighteenth-century authorities suggested that the strains to which the child was subjected caused them any anxiety. None of the great ladies who found the little genius pettable ever suggested that his way of life was unnatural.

Wolfgang was a born musician, incredibly gifted but destined sooner or later to earn his living—probably in a great court under an illustrious patron; if, by the time Wolfgang became an adult, the whole world knew his genius, the greatest posts would be opened to him. At the same time, reasoned his father, the world should have the opportunity to share in the wonder and delight which Leopold found in his son, and the younger Wolfgang was, the greater the sensation he would make. That Leopold could hope to make money from exploiting his son as the greatest of prodigies was, of course, to a meagrely paid court musician an attractive by-product of the scheme.

So the tour went on, with public concerts at which each of the children played solos and took part in duets: Wolfgang was set to play at sight any music produced by members of the audience, and his powers of sight-reading dazzled his hearers. The children would play duets while the keyboards of their instruments were covered by a cloth. Wolfgang improvised. At court in Vienna he played a concerto by the elderly Georg Christoph Wagenseil, whom the little boy wanted to meet and who sat beside him to turn the pages. Maria Theresa petted the little virtuoso, as did the ill-fated Marie Antoinette (two months Wolfgang's senior) whom Wolfgang promised to marry

Maria Theresa and the young Marie Antoinette, who later became Queen of France.

because she helped him to his feet when he had slipped upon the polished floor. Both he and Nannerl were presented with court dress by the Empress (the clothes were the splendid cast-offs of her younger children), and the two were painted in their finery before their departure to Germany. Moritz von Schwind, the painter friend of Schubert, romanticised the scene, showing a majestically maternal Empress holding the magnificently clad little boy high in the air over her lap.

The petting seems to have delighted Wolfgang. When, during a visit to Versailles, he played to Madame de Pompadour and was not rewarded with caresses, he asked Nannerl, 'Who is this woman? She won't kiss me. The Empress kissed me.' Daines Barrington, whose account of Wolfgang's abilities includes a comparison of his gifts with those of other remarkable children, suggested something of the reality of his creative powers when he found the little boy in the mood for improvisation:

I said to the boy, that I should be glad to hear an extemporary Love Song, such as his friend Manzoli might choose in an opera.

The boy (who continued to sit at his harpsichord), looked back with much archness and immediately began five or six lines of a jargon recitative proper to introduce a love song.

He then played a symphony which might correspond with an air to the single word 'Affetto'.

The song, Barrington noted, was properly composed in aria form and was 'really above mediocrity'; it was as long as a typical operatic aria. Barrington's next request, at which the 'boy again looked back with much archness', was for a Song of Rage.

The word 'archness', used by a writer who had the estimable eighteenth-century habit of using the exact words he meant, somehow suggests that the child was precisely and knowingly aware of the impact he made on adults, conscious not only of his abilities but also of the value of an easy and charming manner. Not that Barrington seems to have been in any way put out by the child's knowingness but was apparently completely captivated by a serious eight-year-old musician riding an improvised hobby-horse.

The Mozart family remained in London from 22 April 1764 to 24 July 1765, the visit being extended because during their stay Leopold fell seriously ill. London had been welcoming, but so had Paris and the various German cities that the family had visited on the outward journey. George III, a devoted music-lover whose tastes were a little old-fashioned, heard the two children twice at court soon after their arrival, and Leopold noted in a letter that he actually bowed to them one morning from his coach.

After London came Holland, where the children were both ill, and a return to Paris, where they played at court again, and then back to Salzburg after brief calls at Geneva, Lausanne, Berne, Zürich and Munich. The family remained in Salzburg until September 1767, when they went to Vienna; this was their base until their return to Salzburg in early January 1769.

George III, to whom the Mozart children played when they were staying in London in 1764.

21

Even in his native city, however, Wolfgang was kept busy. Archbishop Schrattenbach found the stories of Wolfgang's talent hard to believe and kept him locked up alone to write the first part of the music to a morality play, *Die Schuldigkeit des ersten Gebotes*, the second part of which was to be written by Michael Haydn, the most recent notable recruit to the Salzburg musical staff. Up to this time the Archbishop had given some of the credit for Wolfgang's reputation to his father; now he knew that Wolfgang could sit down alone and produce performable music. The Archbishop's commission was followed by a piece of funeral music (*Grabmusik*, K. 42) and by an intermezzo, *Apollo et Hyacinthus*.

As a publicity exercise the great tour had been a success. Leopold, Wolfgang and Nannerl had all been seriously ill, but the Mozart children were

London in 1746 by T. Bowles: Leopold purchased some of his engravings when the Mozarts visited the city.

famous. But even without the complication of ill health it would not have earned enough money to make them rich. A concert at Mainz made 200 florins. At Frankfurt the concert that Leopold had planned had been so successful that it had to be followed by others; for playing to George III and Queen Charlotte the reward was 25 guineas. A concert in London on 5 June 1764 had grossed 100 guineas, but the rent of the hall had been 5 guineas; candles and music stands had to be hired

separately; each clavier—one for each child—cost half a guinea; the singers cost 5 or 6 guineas; the leader of the orchestra cost 3 guineas and the rank and file of the orchestra half a guinea each, but most of the musicians gave their services free. The London audience paid willingly to hear the children, and to extract the maximum profit Leopold announced their departure well in advance of its date and arranged small-scale recitals in their lodgings at a cheap rate. Two other appearances at St James's Palace and a final 'farewell' concert at cheap rates made sure that he took all the money he could from England.

Any profits from the tour tended to be swamped by its costs. The courts they visited produced not fees but presents; George III's payment in guineas was not the normal practice for instrumentalists invited to play at court. (Presents could be sold, of course, but preferable were gifts such as that of 25 sequins they received for playing in the palace of Prince Pallavicini in 1770.) 'We have received sundry valuable presents here,' wrote Leopold on 4 November 1763, 'but do not wish to turn them into cash. What with snuff boxes and leather cases and suchlike gewgaws, we shall soon be able to open a stall.' Their experience of London was typical of the finances of the tour: rewards in London were richer than rewards on the Continent, and London's familiarity with public concerts perhaps produced a readier audience, but unavoidable expenses more than matched their additional income.

The endless journey, as it must have seemed to the little boy who enjoyed travelling more than he enjoyed destinations, was Wolfgang's education, bringing him into contact with music and musicians wherever he went. The travels fed his musical nature in an age which still provided music in distinct national or local styles, with strong individual accents, so to speak, within a generally accepted musical language. Wolfgang's musical character, as we have seen, was to compound in his own style whatever he heard that was both new and capable of further expansion until, eventually, the Mozart style became totally comprehensive. In Salzburg the baroque forms lingered, offering a hybrid style in which, in the works of the better composers, German and Austrian traits provided a fruitful conflict. The leading Viennese composers were concerned with the reconciliation of German and Italian musical elements—the contrast between the emotional Italianate melody and the introspective, powerfully contrapuntal style of the north; the eighteenth-century 'gallant' style, courtly and elegant, grew out of this contrast. Salzburg music was primarily vocal and orchestral, and as Nannerl and Mozart showed their gifts first of all as keyboard players, the bulk of the keyboard music available for Leopold and his pupils came from north Germany; it was written in a more instrumental, less extended melodious style than Austrian or Italian music; its harmony was more adventurously expressive. Leopold compiled for the children an anthology of 135 keyboard works arranged in suites according to their key; necessity sent him to the works of north German composers such as Telemann, who had achieved a unification of German seriousness with the mannerisms and techniques of French music, its rhythmic vitality and alertness and its deliberate grace of style, and to the sensational expressiveness of Carl Philipp Emanuel Bach, the most famous of the sons of the great but almost forgotten Johann Sebastian; to his own generation, Carl Philipp Emanuel was the great expressive master of new music. In order to make any sense of his own musical experience Wolfgang from the start had to make some sort of reconciliation between rival styles.

During his first visit to Paris Mozart discovered the music of Johann Schobert, a Silesian composer who had settled in Paris in 1760 at the age of forty and become extremely popular and influential. Schobert's music is graceful, elegantly light in texture and tastefully sentimental. A greater influence, and a better composer, Johann Christian Bach, became Wolfgang's friend in London. Johann Christian was the renegade of the Bach family: born in 1735 he had removed himself entirely from traditional Bach influences and had taken himself to Italy, where he became a Roman Catholic and organist of Milan cathedral, won success as an opera composer and settled in London in 1762 as composer to the opera. The vicissitudes of English opera, however, persuaded him to go into partnership with another expatriate German composer—Carl Friedrich Abel, who had arrived in London three years before his partner and given concerts there. In 1765, a few months after the arrival of the Mozart family, having directed concerts under other auspices Bach and Abel began their own regular, and very influential, series of concerts at which the latest European styles won their first hearing in London. Johann Christian Bach was one of the supreme masters of the 'gallant style'—light, lucid, graceful, charmingly melodious, choosing simplicity and naturalness in preference to learning. J. C. Bach's symphonic style grew directly out of the Italian opera overture, with its three sections expanding into three movements—fast, slow and fast—and exploiting the contrast between a home (tonic) key and its dominant. The middle-aged composer and the little boy struck up a warm friendship. The relationship was playful rather than pedantically that of teacher and learner; Wolfgang would sit on Johann Christian's lap while they improvised together, each answering the other's inventions. Once he had heard Johann Christian's symphonies Wolfgang had to write symphonies of his own, asking Nannerl to remind him to write interesting parts for the horns.

These were Mozart's first orchestral works, and it was in London that the boy produced his first vocal music, a choral work setting the Psalm 'God is our refuge and strength'; he presented the manuscript to the British Museum, calling the piece a madrigal. We do not know what music Wolfgang heard in London, apart from the inescapable Handel, but there is no reason why he should not

A pastel of Johann Christian Bach by Matschlieu.

24

25

'God is our Refuge' was the first piece of choral music written by Mozart. He was nine when he composed it.

have come across compositions by Handel's English contemporaries and successors who maintained the English cathedral music tradition; something of that nature must have prompted him to tackle a biblical text.

Naturally, to Leopold and his son the musical centre of the world was Vienna. The great tour ended in November 1766, but a year later Leopold and the children had returned to Vienna, where Wolfgang's future most probably lay. The time, however, was not opportune; Wolfgang was smitten with smallpox and taken to Brno to recover. When he resumed activity in Vienna, Maria Theresa had given up the throne to her elder son, Joseph II, perhaps the most enlightened and liberal of the benevolent despots, but a man not given to extravagance who had infected the Viennese nobility with an attack of thriftiness. The court was in mourning for the death of Joseph's sister, Princess Maria Josepha, in the smallpox epidemic which had struck first Wolfgang and then Nannerl; therefore there were no public concerts.

Nevertheless, Joseph invited Wolfgang to compose an opera, *La Finta Semplice* (K. 51). An *opera buffa* (realistic comic opera) by a boy of twelve was likely to be a sensation, and therefore a financial success, for reasons possibly quite remote from its musical value. For four years Wolfgang had been waiting for his opportunity to compose an opera, and Daines Barrington's account of his improvised arias show that even at eight the boy knew much about opera and its demands. Mozart's way was to learn things subject to conventions and then to discover how he could handle those conventions in a way that suited him.

But in Vienna the opera was no longer a real state opera dominated by the Emperor and his court. The theatre and the company had been farmed out to a commercial manager, one Affligio, who paid 6000 florins a year for the right to run the theatre in the hope of making a profit. Even the Royal Family, according to a letter by Leopold Mozart written in late January 1768, could not interfere with the opera's day to day management, and Wolfgang was to discover for the first time in his life that to compete against composers who earned their living—and not simply applause, kisses and presents—in the theatre was to find himself faced with implacable, unscrupulous enemies. Leopold wished his son to be treated on the same terms as any other opera composer and to conduct the first performance of his work; the rumour soon spread round Vienna that the orchestra refused to play under a mere child. Singers, to whose requirements Wolfgang had tailored the music in the eighteenth-century custom, apparently decided that they owed it to their dignity to object to the arias they had already praised. Then it was decided that Wolfgang knew too little Italian to do justice to the libretto.

Leopold, fighting for his son with more determination than tact, induced Hasse, the Dresden opera composer, and Metastasio, the Imperial court poet whose libretti had been set over and over again by every composer of standing, to announce that recently they had each heard more than thirty operas in Vienna inferior to *La Finta Semplice*. Leopold invited critics to watch while the unaided Wolfgang set to music arias by Metastasio.

Affligio promised a production but did not begin to prepare it; it seems that to have gone ahead with Wolfgang's work would have been to antagonise the elder composers upon whose output he had to depend to keep the stage occupied, and that to encourage Mozart by pushing on with Joseph II's tactless invitation would have made difficulties later. How much of a consolation it was to the young composer himself that a miniature dramatic work, *Bastien und Bastienne* (K. 50), was produced in the little private theatre of their friend Dr Mesmer we do not know. This was a German version of a French ballad opera already staged in Paris with music selected from popular tunes. Mozart composed it entirely himself, but perhaps because the text was originally in French—a parody of the opera *Le Devin du Village* by the writer Jean-Jacques Rousseau—Wolfgang chose to write in a lyric, songful style close to that of ballad opera; the solo songs are songs, not formal arias, and they adopt the French lyric forms suggested by their words.

As it became clear to Leopold (who seems to have cared much more than his son) that *La Finta Semplice* would not be produced in Vienna, the Imperial family was invited to the first performance of Wolfgang's first complete Mass, written for the dedication of the new chapel of a Vienna orphanage. Though the Offertory composed to be sung in the liturgy on the day of dedication has survived, as K. 47, the Mass itself is probably lost—unless it is really the Mass in C (K. 139), an ambitious work in a properly festal style with an orchestra that includes trumpets, trombones and drums. Köchel, who catalogued Mozart's works and largely established their dates of composition, thought that it was written in Salzburg in 1772. The struggles with Affligio continued, the manager threatening to produce Wolfgang's opera under protest and ensure that it failed, before Leopold would admit defeat. Only then did Leopold, having vastly overstayed his permitted leave, return to his duties in Salzburg. Archbishop Schrattenbach, who might justifiably have been annoyed with his absentee vice-*Kapellmeister*, poured balm on his wounded pride and with great magnanimity ordered a performance of *La Finta*

Semplice for the following 1 May.

The composition of a full-scale Mass had apparently diverted Wolfgang's thoughts to church music. In quick succession, in Vienna and Salzburg, he composed two settings of the *Missa Brevis* (K. 49 and K. 65) and another full-scale Mass (K. 66). Various other works followed, with two cassations (K. 63 and K. 99) and a serenade (K. 100), as well as three sets of minuets (K. 103–105). All this was the sort of music in demand in Salzburg: the repertoire of the cathedral choir needed constant additions. Divertimenti, serenades and cassations were popular social forms demanding less attention than a symphony. The word 'cassation' is a little philological puzzle. Possibly it comes from the Italian word *cassa*, a drum, and thus from the Latin *cassare* to dismiss or march off; in this case a cassation would have been the last item of a jollification. But possibly the word is a corruption of the German *Gasse* (a back street or alley): 'Gasatim Gehen' is the Austrian phrase for wandering round the streets 'chatting up' any available girls. When Mozart's widow was selling his manuscripts to the publisher André nine years after his death, she referred to the works she called *Gassationen* as though that had been Mozart's own term: 'Gassationen', she noted in the margin, 'is an incomprehensible, ugly provincial term.'

In December 1769, after almost a year at home, leaving his wife and daughter behind Leopold set off with Wolfgang for Italy. Heralded by letters of introduction, after a brief stay in Innsbruck they visited Rovereto, Verona, Mantua, Cremona and Milan. The incredulity with which Wolfgang had been greeted in northern Europe was repeated in Italy. He was made to play all his tricks with a hidden keyboard, tackling at sight music new to him, improvising, playing concertos. His own compositions were heard in his programmes and their growing range, technical skill and greater emotional depth, added to childish charm, appealed greatly to his audiences. There was less

of the feeling implied by Daines Barrington that Wolfgang was an incredibly gifted keyboard technician with a remarkable knack of mimicking adult emotion. Wherever he played in public, even on a church organ, he was likely to be mobbed, like a contemporary castrato or a modern pop star. In January 1770 the Accademia Filarmonica of Mantua gave a concert which began and ended with Mozart symphonies, in between which the boy was expected to play all his baffling pianistic tricks and to prove his ability as sight-reader and improviser.

At fourteen it was time for Wolfgang to prove himself capable of survival in the world of practical music-making. His Salzburg compositions already did so, though they had to be played wherever he went to prove the point that he could effectively provide whatever was wanted according to the strict conditions of the period. He had brought with him two concert arias, one for soprano (K. 70) and one for tenor (K. 71); to these, in February and March 1770, he added five more, all for soprano (K. 77, 78, 79, 88 and 143). The texts were by Metastasio, the supreme librettist of *opera seria*. (*Opera seria* is the name given to the solemn, occasionally pompous, style of court opera which takes its characters through danger and trouble to a happy ending.) A composer could not, without a commission, expect an opera to have much chance of being taken up for production by any management; concert arias, each following a prefatory recitative, were a composer's chance to show his aptitude for dramatic composition and they were, too, in demand by singers who for one reason or another—the most common was a concert for their own benefit—had to make a concert appearance. During the rest of his life Mozart wrote about thirty such arias, almost all for specific singers. The 1770 concert arias were, therefore, stating his claim as an opera composer; four of them were heard at a concert in the house of Count Firmian, the Austrian Governor-General of Lombardy, before an audience of unusual social eminence, and they resulted in Wolf-

Padre Giovanni Battista Martini, noted composer and musicologist, of Bologna.

30

Above and left: The boy Mozart, aged about fourteen, seen through the romantic eyes of eighteenth-century Europe. These two unlikely portraits show him with the blond curls and innocent features of an angel.

gang's receiving the commission for an opera to open the next season in the Grand Ducal theatre in Milan.

Leopold, a respectable court composer, made only one condition—the approval of the Prince Archbishop of Salzburg; he did not, in other words, wish to sever any connections in Salzburg which might one day be advantageous to his son. The libretto of the work for Milan was to be sent to Wolfgang wherever he was in Italy; he was to deliver the recitatives in October and to return to Milan in November to work with the singers whose vocal idiosyncrasies and personalities he would need to study if he were successfully to compose the arias. Then he would supervise rehearsals and direct the first performances.

Eighteenth-century operas were written in this way because it was the singers rather than the composer who attracted the audience, and the composer's professional expertise had to include the ability, if not to express himself through the style and idiosyncrasies of singers, at least to make effective use of them. Wolfgang, at fourteen, would be expected to oblige the singers chosen for his work and flatter them by showing off their most impressive tricks.

At Lodi, as father and son left Milan, Wolfgang wrote his first string quartet (K. 80). By 24 March they were in Bologna, where music was not a matter of easy entertainment but of high intellectual standards inherited from the past and presided over by the priest–musicologist–composer Padre Giovanni Battista Martini, the most profound musical scholar of the day. Bologna was to occupy more of their time later in the year, and they moved on to an equally short stay in Florence, where they met the famous composer–violinist Nardini and gave a concert before the Grand Duke of Tuscany. Holy Week they spent in Rome, where Wolfgang wrote a new symphony, K. 81. In the Sistine Chapel he heard the *Miserere* by Allegri, a work for nine-part choir unpublished because since its composition in about 1630 it had been reserved for the use of the Papal Choir; at one time it had been a crime to copy it, though a few copies existed and Dr Charles Burney, the English historian, had been given one which he reproduced in the second volume of his *History of Music*, published in 1782. Wolfgang, at the age of fourteen, apparently noted enough of the work as it was sung to be able to complete the music from memory; Mendelssohn did the same thing in 1830, when he was twenty-one.

After Rome, Leopold and Wolfgang moved to Naples, where a month's stay proved disappointing. The King was not interested though the Queen was attentive, and the first wife of the English Ambassador, Sir William Hamilton (soon to be replaced by the notorious Emma) pleased Leopold by her nervousness when she played to

31

Wolfgang. In Naples there was opera, notably by Niccolo Jommelli, the most famous Italian composer of the day, whose style was more progressive and more adventurous than that of any of his Italian contemporaries.

On the way back through Rome Wolfgang was given the Order of the Golden Spur from the Pope, and by July the Mozarts were back in Bologna, where Padre Martini gave Wolfgang lessons in the strict counterpoint of the sixteenth century, and the boy was offered the examination which would make him a member of the Accademia Filarmonica of Bologna; this was a genuine test of scholarship, and he was set the task of writing a choral work in which he was to use a plainchant antiphon, 'Quaerite primum', as a *cantus firmus*—a set, unvarying bass part to be adorned with parts for soprano, alto and tenor according to the rules of strict counterpoint. The work, listed by Köchel as K. 86, was a test of scholarship rather than of creativity, and it was accepted—though there is some reason to believe that Martini helped Wolfgang to solve its problems; Leopold was characteristically jubilant, for though the exercise was really irrelevant to any aims Wolfgang might have, membership of the Accademia Filarmonica was a mark of genuine scholarship, not a mere courtesy offered to a distinguished, charming and youthful visitor.

In late October, according to his contract with Milan, Wolfgang had dealt with the recitatives of the libretto which had reached him, *Mitridate, Rè di Ponto*. This was an operatic version of a play by Racine, turned into acceptable *opera seria* by Vittorio Amadeo Cigna-Santi. The singers of the company found the young composer to their satisfaction not so much for his high-spirited youthful charm but because he cooperated in every way like a thoroughgoing professional *maestro*. If, nowadays, it is rather beneath a composer's dignity for him to make sure that his music flatters the capability of the performers, the ability to do

so was a necessary part of any eighteenth-century composer's professional equipment. Any composer of fourteen must have learned a lot from close cooperation with experienced performers, and Wolfgang's readiness to oblige must have brought him a great deal of professional expertise. In later years, when he had developed an unrivalled instinct for theatrical effectiveness and an unprecedented power of characterisation through music, there is evidence that he was not always so accommodating towards singers whose horizons were bounded by their view of what they could do effectively.

Mitridate was produced on 26 December, the first night of the season; it was a complete success, repeated twenty times before the season ended in Lent. The Accademia Filarmonica of Verona, not to be outdone by the Bolognesi, elected Wolfgang *Maestro di Capella* when he visited the city in March after a prolonged and oddly lazy stay in Venice, and when he next visited Milan he was met with another commission, for a work to celebrate the marriage of Maria Theresa's son the Archduke Ferdinand to Princess Maria of Modena in the following October. There was time for a return to Salzburg and the composition of some immediately useful music—a *Regina Coeli* (K. 108), the *Litany of Loreto* (K. 109) and a symphony (K. 110)—before he set off for Milan in August to fulfil his second Milan contract. This was for a dramatic serenata, more of a masque or musical than an opera, *Ascanio in Alba*. It was greeted more warmly by the public than the actual opera *Ruggiero* written by the great Dresden veteran Hasse for the occasion. In Padua he had received a commission for a setting of Metastasio's oratorio text *La Betulia Liberata* (K. 118) on which he set to work with another symphony.

On their return to Salzburg on 15 December 1771 vice-*Kapellmeister* Leopold received his full salary for something like four months' work in the previous two years.

3 Mozart and the Eighteenth-century System

In 1771, when the Mozarts returned in triumph from their first trip to Italy, Wolfgang could regard himself as a professional musician capable of doing a composer's work. He was qualified by his achievements, which showed his ability to produce technically correct, acceptable music for any purpose in church, theatre, concert hall or salon. He returned, moreover, to an official post listed in the court calendar as third *Konzertmeister*, required, when called upon to do so, to act as leader–director of the Archbishop of Salzburg's orchestra. The entry in the court calendar for 1769 which names him in this position mentions no pay allotted to him, so it seems that Archbishop Schrattenbach was simply pre-empting his services ready for when they would be required.

Apart from whatever formal teaching Leopold had given to him, Wolfgang had profited from the informal training provided by his travels; this had been ideal for a mind like Wolfgang's, which took in new ideas and applied them to purposes of his own. In this sense he was by the time he was fifteen as fully trained a musician as was likely to be found anywhere in Europe, master of a style in which his innate love of symmetry and grace already synthesised a great variety of local, national and personal characteristics. He had much to learn and a long way to go towards maturity before he became the Mozart who won the adoration of musicians everywhere; but at fifteen he could satisfy the requirements of the average eighteenth-century patron. The danger for him, which we can see but his contemporaries could not, was that he would soon be too busy with routine composition to develop into a composer of masterpieces.

He had grown up in the tradition of eighteenth-century musical craftsmanship. To be a composer was, for Mozart, to be able to write effectively the music that was required to fulfil a commission, to dignify a special occasion or to satisfy a friend. The absence of any demand usually meant that he would take a holiday from composition, not because he was without inspiration but because the actual need for composition had been withdrawn; he lived in a musical world where his function was to satisfy specific demands and, like any craftsman, he was primarily concerned with the technical quality both of his own work and of the music he heard. In the letters he wrote which have been collected into a Mozart family archive, dating from about his fourteenth birthday, he never talked about music in such grandiose terms as the quality of its inspiration. His concern is always the worth of the composition in professional terms; music should be well written, and if it is well written it will be, in his phraseology, effective. When he wrote to his father in 1781 about the composition of *Die Entführung aus dem Serail* he gave no indication that he regarded the duet of his hero and heroine, Belmonte and Constanze, awaiting possible execution in Act Three, as musically more important than the scene in which Pedrillo, Belmonte's servant, makes Osmin, the irascible keeper of the harem, helplessly drunk; both were musical tasks demanding the proper application of the appropriate techniques and both needed to be written with the greatest possible skill: whether the music was 'serious' or 'comic' had nothing to do with its intrinsic quality.

The conscientious professional composer of Mozart's day could hardly adopt a different attitude, for it was his duty to compose what his patron wanted rather than what he himself might wish to write at any given time. Municipalities and noblemen, the most frequent patrons, employed a musical staff and a *Kapellmeister*: the *Kapellmeister's* duty was to see that music was available and prepared for performance whenever it was needed. The day of the freelance had not yet dawned, and the professional composer was a necessary functionary whose contract demanded that he provide music, usually by composing it, whenever an opera, a symphony or a concerto was required, whenever the patron wished to take part in chamber music, whenever his wife wanted a new aria or a new piano piece. The composer would discreetly tailor whatever music he wrote for such people to exploit what abilities they had and to mask their defects. The *Kapellmeister's* contract laid down that anything composed as part of his service to his patron was the patron's property, and he needed to gain special permission to undertake work not for his patron or to sell any of his compositions to a publisher. He was, too, completely tied to his patron and could not resign his position; the only escape from a post in which he was unhappy or dissatisfied was to request his dismissal and to hope that it would be granted; his patron, however, could dismiss him at any time.

The position of a court musician was, in other words, almost feudal. For all the range of his reponsibilities, a *Kapellmeister* was not highly paid. Although someone like Haydn, with an enlightened and liberal patron in Prince Nikolaus Esterhazy, could become famous and eventually rich, Haydns and Prince Nikolauses were uncommon, and the *Kapellmeister* was poorly paid and not socially exalted; rank and file instrumentalists were on equal footing with valets, the *Kapellmeister* with butlers and major-domos.

In Salzburg the Mozarts lived in their own lodgings, not in accommodation provided by the court; thus they avoided a good deal of what the intellectual Leopold would have regarded (as his son was later to do) as uncongenial company. To some extent, therefore, the Mozarts were favoured. Apart from the ease with which Leopold could obtain leave to further his son's career, Wolfgang's Salzburg duties started with a nominal post in order to ensure his services later. This meant that for the time being he could devote his time to composition for the Salzburg court and for its instrumentalists; he could write for the important people of the city when they wanted music with which to celebrate. His new opera for Milan, scheduled for production immediately after Christmas 1772, could wait—as long as its recitatives were ready—until he arrived there to work with the singers. Meanwhile he completed the commissioned *La Betulia Liberata*, eight symphonies and four divertimenti, and set to work on the large-scale, impressive *Litaniae de Venerabili Altaris Sacramento*—all works which could justify his so-far unpaid position in Salzburg, where things were in the process of radical change.

In 1771 the indulgent, easy-going, patriarchal Archbishop Sigismund von Schrattenbach died. In 1772 Hieronymus Count von Colloredo was crowned Prince Archbishop, and the Mozart story found its villain. Schrattenbach had cared little about the many absences of his vice-*Kapellmeister*, or about the way in which Leopold Mozart overstayed his generous leaves; he had not demurred when Leopold, who was not making a fortune from the premature fame of his son, applied for the salary he had not earned. It was plain, and perfectly natural, that Leopold cared more for Wolfgang's future career than for the duties of his official position; quite possibly Schrattenbach himself, like so many others, had been charmed by the gifted child. The unpaid *Konzertmeister* was now sixteen years old, and he had been admired and possibly spoiled by almost everybody he had met. It is less easy to love a gifted adolescent than to dote upon a charming little boy.

Colloredo was a man of his time, a product of the Enlightenment who read and admired the writings of Voltaire and Rousseau; as a rationalist, eager for reform in society and religion, he could not sympathise with a vice-*Kapellmeister* who expected the privilege of long leaves during which he attended to private business while receiving his pay. If we have called Colloredo the villain of the Mozart story, the faults that made him so were not all on one side. Genius or not, Colloredo expected Wolfgang to take his place in the hierarchy and to do the work that he was supposed to do; he turned Wolfgang's post into a normally paid position with a salary of 150 florins a year and, it may be, congratulated himself on regularising the position of the most gifted of his musicians. It was Wolfgang's music—another dramatic serenata, *Il Sogno di Scipione* (Scipio's Dream, K. 126)—which was chosen to provide the music for the first big court occasion of the new reign two months after the new Archbishop's enthronement. The text was old; it had been written for the name-day of the Emperor Charles V in 1735 and provided with new music for the name-day of Francis I eight years later.

Colloredo, in most respects a liberal, cultured and enlightened man, seems to have lacked humanity. Leopold Mozart was the sort of musician he might find anywhere, conscientious, thorough but in no way outstanding. Wolfgang, of course, was a feather in his cap—young, gifted and internationally famous. But Colloredo could not see that the younger Mozart had been more or less drafted into his service, had never applied for his post and was unlikely to settle down happily to the sort of musical life Salzburg could offer him. His salary of 150 florins per annum paid in monthly instalments was very low; there was no regular opera, and the court orchestra shortly before had apparently been notable for the roughness and coarseness of its tone. A minimum of imagination would have shown Colloredo that Wolfgang would outgrow Salzburg, but the Archbishop was not so much interested in enabling the youth to fulfil his ambitions as in teaching both the Mozarts that rules were meant to be obeyed. Wolfgang was well known outside Salzburg and from time to time in demand in greater capitals. Colloredo set out to make it increasingly difficult for him to accept commissions and make appearances away from Salzburg. It was not hard, he found, to drive the boy, who had a clear, even arrogant sense of his own worth, into rebellion. Leopold might grumble at the clipping of his wings but, in his fifties, he could hope for no better position than the one he held at Salzburg.

On 4 September 1776 Wolfgang sent a copy of an Offertory (*Misericordias Domini*, K. 222) to Padre Martini in Bologna; in an accompanying letter he told his elderly friend that Leopold, after thirty-six years' service at the Salzburg court, had nothing to hope for because 'the present Archbishop cannot and will not do anything for people who are getting on in years'. In future Leopold could only endure whatever difficulties Colloredo made for him. In so far as the main purpose of all the family travels in Wolfgang's childhood had been to advance his claims to a senior position at a court musically advanced enough, and rich enough, fully to exploit his gifts, it had taken for granted a future in which the Prince Archbishop was as easy-going as Schrattenbach. With Colloredo showing himself to be totally unsympathetic to servants whom he regarded as too conceited to take their proper place, an occasional absence was seen as a definite attempt to secure a new appointment; but any search for a better life depended upon his permission to travel. An invincible force was moving towards an immovable object, if not rapidly at least inevitably.

There was, of course, always enough work to do in Salzburg. The year 1773 saw the composition of six divertimenti and three symphonies, among which, late in the year, was the passionate No. 25 in G minor (K. 183), the first of Wolfgang's important works to be written in a minor key. Most of the following year was spent in Salzburg, during which Mozart built up his dislike for the Archbishop's musical establishment while writing the sort of music it needed. The Bassoon Concerto (K. 191), two settings of the *Missa Brevis* (K. 192 and K. 194), three further symphonies (K. 200–202) and the Serenade in D major (K. 203) were the accompaniment to his post as *Konzertmeister*.

The bulk of Mozart's church music was written in these Salzburg years; after he had left the city for good in 1781, he wrote no church music except for the glorious but unfinished Mass in C minor

Mozart's letter to his mother, written from Munich on 14 January 1775, telling her of the success of his opera La Finta Giardiniera.

Gottlob! Meine opera ist gestern als den 13 ten in scena München d 14 [ten] Jäner

gegangen; und so gut niedergestellen, daß ich der Mama den lärmen 1775
ohnmöglich beschreiben kan. Erstens war das ganze Theater so gestoßt voll,
daß schon leute wieder zurück haben müßen. Nach einer jeden Aria war jederzeit
ein erschröckliches getös mit glatschen, und viva maestro geschryen. Ihro durchleucht
die Churfürstin, und die verwittibte, (: welche mir vis à vis waren :) sagten
mir auch bravo. Wie die opera aus war, so ist unter der Zeit so lange still
ist, bis das ballet anfangt, nichts als geklätscht und geschryen worden; bald
aufgehört. Bald wieder angefangen, und so fort. Nach dem bin ich mit meinem
papa in ein gewißes Zimmer gegangen, wo der Churfürst, und die ganze
hof durch muß, und hab s: d: dem Churfürst und Churfürstin und der hohheit
die Hand geküßt, welche alle sehr gnädig waren; so mal zu aller früh
gieng. s: fürstlichen bischof in Chiemsee her, und ließt mir gratuliren,
daß die opera bey allen so unvergleichlich ausgefallen ist; Ihnen versichere
euch, Daß die Mama es gar ein Gott [weiß] nicht
wie wenden noch sich gewiß ... träum. Nun müste und noth-
wendige ursache ist, weil die heutigen frühen die opera erdenken
geben und, und ich gehe nothwendig bey der production bin --- sonst
würden Weg sie nicht mehr kommen --- daß ich ihro
curios seine. ich küße der Mama 1000 mahl die Händ. Meine kamerad
mein gute freund und freundinn. an M: Andretter mein Compliment.
ich bitte ihr um verzeihung daß ich noch nicht geantwort, aber ich

hatte ohnmöglich Zeit, mit nächstem soll es geschehen. Adieu. in hinberl
1000 bußerln

and the equally glorious but unfinished *Requiem*, and the *Ave Verum*. This drying up of what had been a constant flow from Salzburg of works for the Catholic liturgy has been seen by some writers as the relinquishment of an unwanted task. The so-called 'worldliness' of the earlier church music has been cited to prove Mozart's growing lack of sympathy with the Catholic Church as he became acquainted with the solemnities of Freemasonry, but there is no suggestion that he found his Masonry seriously incompatible with his Catholic upbringing, although it seems that Masonic ceremonial struck him as more vivid and immediate than the familiar Catholic ritual.

Mozart however, as we have seen, was a professional composer providing music as and when it was needed. Once he had left Salzburg the demand for church music dried up until, six months before his death, the *Requiem* was commissioned. The C minor Mass he wrote as a thank-offering for his marriage, and it remains unfinished because other music was needed and it had to be laid aside so that he could earn his living.

The Mass, to Mozart, was a definite musical form in which the composer must work; in what is generally known as the 'Viennese' Mass the formulation of public worship presented composers with a discipline they must more or less strictly observe. The Gloria and the Credo, for example, end in fugues, while the Agnus Dei, which opens as a slow movement in a minor key, turns in its last petition into the major and becomes a happy *allegro* in the interest of what the eighteenth century regarded as a musically satisfying conclusion. Such considerations weighed more on any composer's mind than the entirely subjective notions of 'worldliness' or 'theatricality' for which Mozart's and other eighteenth-century settings of the Mass have been condemned. Mozart's concern was whether the music

Sigmund Haffner was a wealthy Salzburg businessman for whose family Mozart composed the Serenade K. 250 and the well-known Haffner Symphony.

was good, and by that he meant whether it had clarity, inventiveness and technical precision.

Whatever expressive problems are integral to the composition of the setting of the Mass were intensified in Salzburg by a decree of Archbishop Colloredo. Mozart explained to Padre Martini that a solemn Mass, with all its rich ceremonial, should be given a full musical setting with an orchestra that included trumpets and percussion, but that this full setting should not continue for longer than forty-five minutes. The Masses which Mozart composed between the end of 1772 and his departure from the Archbishop's service are works designed with remarkable skill to combine the proper grandeur of the ritual with the economy of style upon which Colloredo insisted. This meant that the vocal soloists were used most often as a solo ensemble offering a textural contrast to the full choral passages. The Gloria and Credo became passages of choral declamation in which the orchestra is concerned with the quasi-symphonic development of orchestral themes. In this respect Mozart's Salzburg Masses are intensely thoughtful, intelligent solutions to specific musical problems.

A commission from the Munich court (which not even Colloredo could obstruct) took Wolfgang to Munich in 1775 for the production of a new *opera buffa*, *La Finta Giardiniera* (The Pretended Garden Girl), which was produced on 13 January 1775. This was a better work than the earlier *La Finta Semplice*: its text produced fewer artificial complications and dealt with characters rather than with types, and it offered the composer a more genuine range of emotion to deal with. Mozart gave its orchestra a richer treatment than audiences of Italianate *opera buffa* were used to, but he saw to it that the voices were treated naturally and given extremely effective music to sing.

By March, however, he was back in Salzburg working on a new Salzburg opera, *Il Rè Pastore* (The Shepherd King), to be produced for the visit of the Emperor's brother, the Archduke Maximilian. This gave a composer little opportunity for anything but grateful vocal writing and effective orchestration; the libretto was by Metastasio, and it was designed as a meditative poem about the innate authority of monarchy, the divine order which monarchy represents, and the natural integrity of a lawful king. Mozart made no effort to unfreeze its conventions into lively drama but turned it into a series of splendid arias of great beauty, though little individual character.

Colloredo, incidentally, visited Munich during the run of *La Finta Giardiniera* and was congratulated on his luck in having the services of a composer of Wolfgang's ability. Leopold, telling the story in a letter to his wife of 18 January, says that the Archbishop simply shook his head and shrugged his shoulders.

The duties of his Salzburg post were apparently responsible during 1775 for the composition of five violin concertos which, it seems, Wolfgang himself played. Less complex in form and less dazzling in inventive power than the great piano concertos which were to follow his departure from Salzburg, each of the violin concertos seems to express not only the composer's high-spirits, his sensitivity to emotion and his delight in forms worked out with his personal combination of surprise and impeccable logic; each seems to define the essential personality of the violin itself.

In July 1776 Sigmund Haffner's daughter was married; the great businessman commissioned a serenade from Wolfgang to mark the occasion. The Serenade (K. 250) with its introductory march (K. 249), became the biggest and most sumptuous of the works Mozart wrote for such occasions, its central movements comprising a violin concerto within the normal serenade pattern of quick movement, minuet, slow movement, minuet and finale. The music is easy, natural and beautiful, with Mozart's unstrained naturalness of emotion. Three Masses followed; these were not, apparently, specifically commissioned but were sure to have been heard, as was a new Litany (K. 243). The Countess Lodron and her daughters commissioned a piano concerto for

three soloists and received the Concerto in C (K. 242), and in the following year a French virtuoso visiting Salzburg, a Mademoiselle Jeunehomme about whom nothing else is known, was given Mozart's first completely mature piano concerto (K. 271). Actually, Mozart's title uses the word 'Clavicembalo', which in his usage means harpsichord, and the recipient seems to have been notable both as a technician and as an interpretative artist. The G minor Symphony (K. 183) seems to any listener to be an entirely personal statement, rebellious, passionate, almost over-intense, transgressing eighteenth-century notions of politeness in its anger. The E flat Concerto for Mademoiselle Jeunehomme is equally personal but has a greater variety of mood than the symphony; it has a slow movement which laments some tragedy of its own, and a rondo finale which stormily allows tempo markings of *andantino* and *andante* inside its main *presto* tempo. The episodes suggest that some conflict is in progress; their tendency is to attempt to pull the music into minor keys, but the almost savage energy of the *presto* drives the music on to a fierce, triumphant conclusion.

Another visitor to Salzburg was the Bohemian soprano Josefa Dusek, and her visit produced a concert aria, 'Ah, lo previdi' (K. 272). Josefa was the wife of Franz Dusek, a notable pianist and composer, and the two became friends of Mozart for the rest of their lives. On the evidence of the aria Josefa Dusek was a powerfully dramatic singer, and when Mozart coached his sister-in-law Aloysia Lange (his first great love) in this aria he tried to teach her to treat the work not as song but as drama.

Until the September of 1777 Mozart continued producing the kind of work that Salzburg could use, notably church music, which was all the Arch-

A letter from Wolfgang to Nannerl, written from Naples on 19 May 1770. In it he says: 'I very much like the twelfth minuet of Haydn ... and you have set the bass to it exceedingly well ... You must try your hand at such things more often.'

Cara sorella mia.   Neapel il 19 maggio 1770

alla vostra lettera non saprei veramente rispondere, perché non
av̍ete scritta niente quasi. i Meruetti del Sig: Haiden Vi man-
derò quando alrò via tempo, il primo miest di Map? dai. ma

Vi prego di scrivermi presto,
e tutti i giorni, io Vi ringrazio, di avermi
mandato questi [Hekenhistorien], e Vi prego, se
mai volete aver siel di festa, da mandarmi ancor
ane poco di questi [Fuchtnu]. perdonate mi che scrivo
sò malamente, ma la ragione è perchè anche io hebbi
un poco mal di testa. Den Baso betteni Menuet von
[...] und [...] gefällt mir nicht
wohl, und den Bass seyt [...] darzu
Componirt, und [...] Anftnu, sind ich bitten
[...] zu [...] spielen: den meine soll
nicht [...] die [...] zu zhm
zu [...]: schreibu mir, wie es den H: Canari geht,
[...] die noch [...] oder noch [...] darzu [...]
[...] den Canari drucken. spiel in eusern wohnzimmer
[...] den lehnu mir [...] den eusern. a propos
der H: Johanes [...] euern gratulations [...]
uber [...] und die sie [...] schreibn sollnu,
[...] nider [...] doch
werdu ich ihms schon [...] den lies sie zu Salzburg, was darinn stehen sollnu. unseren
[...] die eusern [...] Compliz [...]
wir [...] sie [...] mugu[...] sie [...] den
[...] nicht [...] mehr [...]
adio [...]

Wolfgang Mozart

42

bishop seemed regularly to require of him— another ground for discontent to add to his patron's chilly lack of appreciation and the restricted musical life of Salzburg. It was clear that there was no real future for Colloredo's third *Konzertmeister*, and on 1 August Wolfgang followed two unanswered petitions for leave which Leopold had sent with one of his own, asking that he and his father be allowed to travel. Leopold may have drafted this third petition, but its hardly veiled impertinence appears to go beyond anything that Leopold might have risked; Leopold would probably have objected to the idea of instructing the Archbishop on the Christian child's duty to his parents. 'The greater the talents which children have received from God', the petition points out, 'the more they are bound to use them for the improvement of their own and their parents' circumstances, so that they may at the same time assist them and take thought for their future progress. The Gospel teaches us to use our talents in this way.' Colloredo's reply indicates that he realised the impertinence: through his court chamberlain he replied, 'In the name of the Gospel, father and son have my permission to seek their fortune elsewhere.' The prospect of unemployment seems to have terrified Leopold; the thought of relinquishing his post made him ill, so that Wolfgang's journey in search of suitable work, through Munich and Mannheim to Paris, saw the twenty-one-year-old youth escorted by his mother. Leopold organised their activities, so far as he was able from Salzburg. In nagging, anxious letters the worried father attempted to make sure that everything he thought should be done was done. He was devoted to his wife, but she seemed to have little ability to deal with anything beyond her household tasks; his son he adored, but he could see that Wolfgang was at times rash and headstrong, ready to take foolish risks. It was necessary for Leopold to keep full control of Wolfgang's affairs; in all the other journeys the direc-

Maria Anna Thekla, Mozart's 'little cousin', with whom he stayed in Augsburg in 1778 while on tour.

tor–father had been on the spot to deal with problems as they arose and to make whatever decisions were necessary. In the past it had seemed a waste of time to bother Wolfgang with practical decisions: the boy existed to make music, and Leopold could spend his less valuable time in planning and organisation. Leopold had brought up his son to leave practical arrangements to others.

The Mozart of these years remains mysterious; we know him as a musician, not as a young man. His compositions seem to stand outside his own experience, as though he composed music about music rather than about the life he knew. The 'little' G minor Symphony (K. 183) and the E flat Piano Concerto (K. 271) seem in no way to tell us directly about his personality. His church music responds to its text, as do his Salzburg dramatic and semi-dramatic works and the choruses he wrote in 1773 for Gebler's play *Thamos, König in Aegypten* (staged in Salzburg in 1779), which apparently drew his attention for the first time to the grandeurs and solemnities of the ancient world.

What little we know of the young man's mind we learn from his letters, and the letters that have survived were written when he was away from home. According to Emily Anderson, editor and translator of the family correspondence, Wolfgang's first recorded letter was written in Salzburg when he was thirteen; it concerns, with some effort to show off, his knowledge of Latin and is addressed to a girl apparently of his own age. From time to time Wolfgang supplemented his father's thorough accounts of their activities; Nannerl is given messages to deliver to friends, often girl friends, in a way which suggests that the boy led a reasonably active social life when he was at home. From these letters we get the feeling that Wolfgang was unduly susceptible and quite likely to injure his future career by a rash, precipitate marriage. At twenty he was still, except in music, a child; he had never been left to make a single practical decision and was apparently happy to leave all such matters to his father so long as he could compose, play and, off duty, enjoy himself. The suspicion that his friends were carefully vetted is unavoidable; this and the increasing uncongeniality of life in Salzburg may well be the reason why Wolfgang's inner life in the 1770s seemed to many biographers to be shadowy and mysterious. It may be that a life dominated by his father's anxious care was in itself the cause of such unusual and deeply personal works as the early G minor Symphony and the remarkable E flat Piano Concerto.

From September 1777, when he set off from Salzburg with his mother, the letters flow. They demonstrate a passion for words, for comic rhymes, for grotesque nicknames, for verbal high spirits. Del Prato, the castrato singer who sang the part of Idamante in the first production of *Idomeneo*, an apparently unteachable singer with nothing in his favour but a good voice, is referred to as *'mio molto amato castrato del Prato'*. His last journey in 1791 finds him devising comic names for his travelling companions or making up pointless rhymes for the fun of it. Scenery and places he rarely noticed, but the people he met inspired him to vivid, shrewd description.

There is much in the letters to surprise us. Mozart's music is a combination of invincible energy with enormous intellectual control and precise elegance. Readers of his correspondence who expect his prose to display the same qualities are surprised to find, as well as the shrewdness, the sensitivity to people, the wit and impetuosity, a man who took the eighteenth century at its face value. In 1771 he saw an execution in Milan and took a cool academic interest in the event. He mentioned it to his mother and sister. 'They hang them here just as they do in Lyons', he noted, with no sense of horror or revulsion. Even more shocking is his mention of the death of Voltaire in his letter to his father written in Paris on 3 July 1778: 'That Godless arch-rascal Voltaire has pegged out like a dog, like a beast. That is his reward.'

Mozart shows a streak of coarseness in his letters that was shared by the whole family—indeed it was probably common to his race and age. The 1778 tour had halted at Augsburg, where Wolfgang and his mother stayed with Leopold's bookbinder brother. Wolfgang was pleased to meet his *'Bäsle'*, little cousin, who seems to have taken his affection more seriously than he meant it. For some time afterwards he wrote her letters of the sort one expects to find only as lavatory graffiti. Cousin Maria Anna Thekla apparently aroused Leopold's suspicions by sending Wolfgang her portrait; her letters, apparently, did not deal in indecencies although nothing in them suggests that she found Wolfgang's coarseness distasteful. And to read them is to realise that though Wolfgang liked his little cousin, he was not in any way attracted to her as a lover is to a possible mistress.

4 Independence

Early in the morning of 23 September 1777 Mozart and his mother set off on their journey, reaching Munich on the afternoon of the following day. In January 1779 he returned alone to Salzburg and within a day or two petitioned the Archbishop for the post of court organist, vacant and waiting for him for more than a year. The tour had cost his mother's life and had secured no practical advantage, though it had brought him into direct and almost entirely friendly contact with the orchestra and composers of the Elector Palatine at Mannheim, exponents of a brilliant virtuoso style of playing and pioneers of German opera. He had experienced his first serious love affair and watched it fade away. Of the works he had composed only a handful seem to modern listeners to be of great importance.

Leopold had directed operations from afar and Wolfgang had obediently accepted orders, but with less alacrity than Leopold would have liked; he had courted the right noblemen, delivered the correct letters of introduction and had done his best to act as Leopold wished. From Munich to Mannheim and on to Paris he had put forward his claims to a good position; almost everybody had supported his applications, but there was no vacancy for him and his youth was against him: he was too young for a senior post and should (so the Elector of Bavaria thought) travel in Italy, studying there to fulfil his brilliant promise. The Court Intendant at Munich, Count Seeau, suggested that he might be able to earn enough money as a freelance in the Bavarian capital to live comfortably if a small official subsidy were added, and thus he could make himself indispensable to Bavarian music and wait for the sort of post that he needed and deserved. Other friends, not involved in court life, suggested that ten wealthy citizens should be found to subsidise Wolfgang to the tune of a ducat a month each,

Right: A view of eighteenth-century Mannheim, where Mozart first met the Weber family in 1778.
Previous page: A medallion of Mozart at the age of twenty-one.

in addition to which Count Seeau could arrange a payment of 200 gulden a year—a third of the private support suggested—and his problems would be over. The scheme apparently appealed to him, but any scheme appealed to him and any scheme seemed practical. 'If we have had to live in Salzburg on 504 gulden,' he wrote, 'surely we could live in Munich on 600 or 800?'

The Elector gave Wolfgang an audience, greeted him in a friendly way, listened to his account of his career but firmly insisted that there was no vacancy the young man could fill. Wolfgang's letters suggested that the Elector annoyed him by treating him as if he were no different from any other run of the mill composer. 'He had no idea what I can do,' Wolfgang wrote to Leopold. '...I am willing to submit to a test. Let him get together all the composers in Munich, let him even summon a few from Italy, France, Germany, England and Spain. I undertake to compete with any of them in composition.' Friends advised him to stay in Munich without an appointment, write four German operas a year and wait on events. He waited, however, only until the court left the capital and then, after a week, obeyed his father's instructions and moved on. Leopold had carefully analysed the plan to find a group of private patrons and proved it to be impractical; what conditions could he make with such a group? How could he reconcile their almost inevitably conflicting claims?

Their next stop was Augsburg, where his uncle introduced him to the city governor and he visited the piano maker, Stein, whose instruments delighted him. So apparently did the company of his little cousin the *Bäsle*. On 16 October he gave a concert with the local orchestra in its regular series, and on 22 October he gave a public concert on his own account. It began and ended with two of his symphonies and included his Concerto for three pianos (K. 242), a C minor Fantasy for piano and two sonatas. These two events brought him 100 florins, from which the expenses of the concert had to be met. On the platform he wore the Order of the Golden Fleece, and suffered some mockery from the younger generation for doing so; the mockery seems to have been intensified by the fact that he took it badly. There was, of course, no position to be found in Augsburg, so the two moved on.

Frau Mozart was already ailing by the time they reached Mannheim on 30 October. Two months later the Elector Carl Theodor inherited the throne of Bavaria and moved his court and most of his musical establishment to Munich, but both musical and personal reasons seem to have made it impossible for Mozart, who had again failed to secure an appointment, to tear himself away and press on to his next hope in Paris. Back in Salzburg, Leopold found this lack of urgency in his son's conduct not only disappointing but incomprehensible.

The musical reason for Wolfgang's readiness to stay in Mannheim was the quality of the Mannheim orchestra, the friendliness of most of the senior musicians and their pioneer work for the cause of serious German opera as distinct from *Singspiel*, German light opera, a form closer to English ballad opera which had considerable popularity in north Germany. Mozart's operatic ambitions were for fully composed opera in which music itself conveyed the essential drama and action irrespective of the language in which it was written. The popular works which he had heard in Munich had left him, he told his father in a letter, 'aching to write an opera', and the ache was intensified by German opera in Mannheim, where libretti dealt with serious, mythological or historical themes and composers were developing a German equivalent to Italian *opera seria* in a style that would reflect German musical tradition and German national tastes. Anton Schweitzer's *Alceste*, the work of the musical director of a company based in Weimar, and *Günther von Schwarzburg*, by the veteran Mannheim composer Ignaz Holzbauer, opened his eyes to opportunities of which he had so far been unaware, even though the Weimar work, as music and as drama, seemed to

Wolfgang to be at best negligible; he was excited by new ideas which he hoped to have an opportunity of exploiting.

Opera in Mannheim, however, though it was progressive in its use of the German language for serious, heroic works, was less important than orchestral music. The Mannheim opera, some people held, existed only in order to give Carl Theodor an excuse for recruiting ballet dancers and female singers into a harem; the Mannheim orchestra, on the other hand, had virtually been created by the Bohemian composer Johann Stamitz, who had become a violinist in the Elector's orchestra in 1741. On becoming *Kapellmeister* Stamitz had built the orchestra into a team of virtuosi playing symphonies and concertos in the new German manner; it became the leading exponent of the latest, most advanced musical style. The Mannheim composers—and among the orchestral players were several whose reputations spread far and wide—pioneered the four-movement symphony, adding the minuet as a contrasting third movement, specialising in types of music which demanded the utmost precision in ensemble, and making such use of startling *crescendi* and *diminuendi* that for a long time these devices were treated as Mannheim inventions. Ignaz Holzbauer became *Kapellmeister* in 1753; he was succeeded as composer by the Italian Niccolò Jommelli. The *Kapellmeister* at the time of Mozart's visit was Christian Cannabich, a composer who poured out a prolific flood of music in all forms. The English historian of music, Charles Burney, touring Europe to gather information for his *History of Music* in the early 1770s (he visited Mannheim in 1773) described the orchestra as 'an army of generals, equally fit to plan a battle as to fight it'.

'The orchestra is excellent and very strong,' wrote Wolfgang to his father after hearing it at High Mass on All Saints' Day, 1777. 'On either side there are ten or eleven violins, four violas, two oboes, two flutes and two clarinets, two horns, four violin cellos, four bassoons and four double-basses, also trumpets and drums.' But he would not have liked to hear his Masses in the Mannheim chapel, because although Mass at Mannheim had to be as compact musically as that at Salzburg, the choir was only twenty strong and vocally poor. The woodwind, however, was outstanding, more accurate in intonation than orchestral woodwind elsewhere; Mozart gave his Oboe Concerto in C (K. 314), written earlier in the year for the Salzburg first oboist Giuseppe Ferlendis, to the Mannheim oboist Ramm, who was an admirable player. But the real excitement was the Mannheim clarinet playing; the clarinet was a new instrument to Mozart, and at Mannheim he began a lifelong love-affair with the instrument, fascinated by its emotional ambiguity, its high spirits at the top of the register and its natural melancholy lower in the range. He was encouraged to play his keyboard works, to give lessons and to write for his pupils. He directed the court orchestra in some of his own works, and set to work on a Sinfonia Concertante for woodwind and orchestra. A wealthy Dutch amateur asked him for a group of pieces—two quartets with flute replacing first violin—and three concertos. But he did not like the flute as a solo instrument: one of the concertos was merely a skilful adaptation of the earlier Oboe Concerto, and his Dutch patron understandably cut down the promised fee by half. Three concert arias, five violin sonatas and two piano sonatas were commissioned and written. It would be a good idea, he told his father, to get the Elector to commission a German opera from him and to remain in Mannheim until the Elector could not do without him; he clearly believed that if he composed a major work for the Mannheim theatre the Elector would approve of it.

Leopold's letters in reply grow increasingly troubled. Wolfgang was enjoying himself in the new world of Mannheim music, where he moved independently, doing as he thought best. He was behaving as though money did not concern him. Leopold wrote on 11 February 1778:

The purpose of your journey was two-fold, either to get a good permanent appointment, or to go to some big city where large sums of money can be earned. Both plans were designed to assist your parents and help your dear sister, but above all to build up your own name and reputation in the world. . . . It depends on your good sense and your way of life whether you die as an ordinary musician or as some famous *Kapellmeister* of whom posterity will read— whether, captured by some woman, you die bedded in straw in an attic full of starving children or whether, after a Christian life spent in contentment, honour and love, you leave the world with your family well provided for and your name respected by all.

In the previous December Wolfgang had announced that he intended to wait in Mannheim till March, though nothing of practical value could be achieved in Mannheim, and then make his way to Paris with Ramm and three other members of the Elector's orchestra who were not accompanying their Prince to Munich. Leopold, already grumbling about Wolfgang's disastrously long stay in Mannheim, told his son that he was too easily taken in by kind-hearted, well-meaning people whose convenience he considered before his own. Having no money—though he could have covered his and his mother's day to day expenses by teaching—he had drawn on his father's account and plunged Leopold into debt.

'I could not let you travel alone', grumbled Leopold, 'as you were not accustomed to attend to everything and to be independent of the help of others.' Wolfgang knew nothing of foreign currencies, he continued; he could not even pack and did not know how to arrange journeys. So the expenses of the tour had to be increased by sending his mother to look after him. At the same time Wolfgang, while seizing every chance to make money, must not be impatient enough to imagine that at the age of twenty-two he could walk at once into a senior post. Paris was important because it was a great city, and properly prepared, making full use of letters of introduction, the visit

to Paris which was so casually put off could have made his fortune.

Wolfgang's answers to his father's worries were childlike and charming; apparently he did not understand why his father was so anxious. He wrote happily of the people he met and the music he heard; he described the compliments he received and the effect of his music on the people who heard it as though this proved that he was doing everything in his power to solve the practical questions—though it is clear that he did not realise what they were. Apparently he believed that loving filial letters would appease his father simply because he did not understand what his father's complaints were about, and the gloomy notes about money slipped easily in one ear and out at the other. Leopold, realising that Wolfgang on his own would do nothing of practical value for himself or for the family, was relieved to find an opportunity of drawing his son back to Salzburg in a position of increased seniority. Adlgasser had died, leaving the post of court organist vacant, and Leopold pointed out to Count Arco, the court chamberlain, that Wolfgang, though busy and courted wherever he went, was still without a regular post. He told his son that Count Arco and several other important officials were anxious for him to accept the post, while many friends in town were eager to have him back as a teacher and composer. The Archbishop's feelings were not described, perhaps because Colloredo had no real opinion but perhaps too because Leopold preferred not to bring Wolfgang's *bête noire* into consideration. Leopold was not above giving a glowing picture of a new post in Salzburg if by doing so he could save his son from an extravagant and unprofitable life.

It is, perhaps, fashionable now to decry Leopold's bourgeois, carefully practical attitude. But Leopold was apparently of the same mind as

Aloysia Lange (née Weber) was a well-known singer with whom Mozart fell in love when she was sixteen. His plans for their future came to nothing, however, and it seems unlikely that she took his passion very seriously.

Brecht in believing that man must eat before he thinks, and must be in a position to eat before he is in a position to compose music. Leopold, who had previously done all he could for his son on the minimum of money without falling into debt, was naturally agitated by Wolfgang's failure to understand his own problems.

On 17 January 1778 the worst news of all reached the worried father: Wolfgang had fallen hopelessly in love. Leopold had noticed before that his son liked the company of girls and was inclined to flirt with them. First there had been a young singer in Munich, who had easily displaced his Salzburg girl friend—the daughter of the court baker, who, hearing that Wolfgang was about to leave home, had abandoned the convent to which she had committed herself believing that her presence in Salzburg would be enough to change his mind; they had danced together but apparently nothing more than that. Then, wrote Leopold, cataloguing his son's fickleness and flirtations, came Maria Anna Thekla, the *Bäsle*; she had taken Wolfgang seriously enough to send her portrait to await him in Salzburg. Then, in Mannheim, there had been the daughter of Christian Cannabich, to whom Wolfgang had given lessons and whose musical portrait he had painted in the slow movement of the Piano Sonata K. 309. Now, Leopold heard, it was Aloysia Weber's turn.

In Mannheim Wolfgang had met the family of Fridolin Weber, one of the musicians who planned to share the journey to Paris; he was uncle of the composer Carl Maria von Weber, bass singer, prompter and copyist at the Mannheim theatre. He had four daughters: Josefa, a soprano in the Mannheim opera and Aloysia, aged sixteen and beginning a career that was to be far more successful than her elder sister's; Constanze, aged fourteen and studying singing, and Sophie, the baby of the family, were too young to interest Mozart. Aloysia was attractive and very talented, but her ambition and the possibility that Mozart might help her to advance it meant more to her than the young composer's adoration. On 4 February Wolfgang told Leopold that he would abandon the journey to Paris and go with Aloysia to Italy, where she could establish her reputation. He would keep himself by composing and playing the piano. In Italy there was always a market for new operas. The question of position and a regular salary seemed to have passed from his mind; he wanted to write operas and be with Aloysia, and this seemed to be his opportunity to do both.

Leopold would not listen; with some justification he pointed out that since Wolfgang was a tiny child he had sacrificed any career of his own to give his son a fair chance of greatness, and that he had found himself heavily in debt since Wolfgang had been left to explore his prospects unsupervised. The disillusioned letters between the two seem to have clarified Wolfgang's mind: his affection for his father appeared to be just as great, but with Leopold far away in Salzburg it was possible for him to think for himself. He had no objection to teaching or to any other way of making money, but for him to teach was to do a favour to the gifted pupil; all but the gifted were a waste of his time and he would not keep appointments with those who expected him to sit and wait until they were ready for a lesson. He was a composer, born to be a *Kapellmeister*, and other work was less than he deserved.

Leopold worked up a considerable degree of jealousy over his son's love for Aloysia. Would Wolfgang always abandon established friends whenever he met someone new, as he was willing to abandon them, and his parents, for the sake of Aloysia? Why did he behave as though life were simply a romantic novel? Was it not time that he began to think of his parents and his sister, and the sacrifices they had made on his behalf? If he really wanted to help Aloysia, the correct, effective way was first to get a good position, make a lot of money, and then go to Italy to write operas; when his operas were in demand, he could insist that managers engaged his favourite soprano. It is clear from Leopold's letters that the dis-

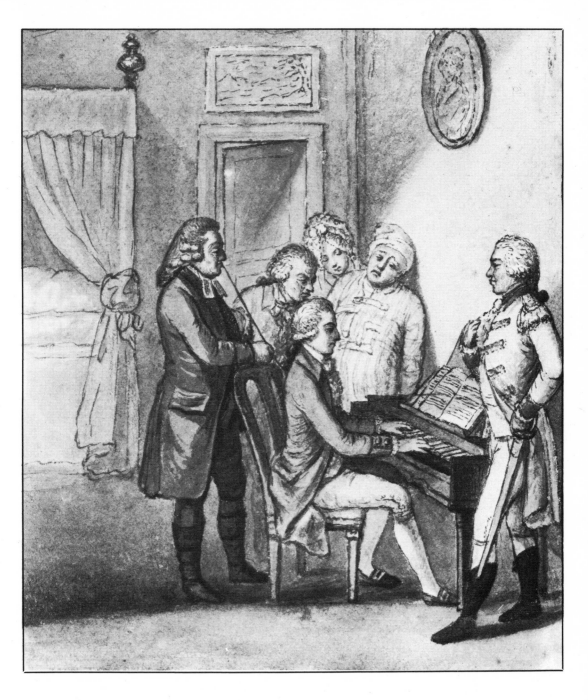

A pen and ink drawing by C. Schütz of Mozart at the piano, with a group of friends in Salzburg.

appointed father was not able to see much virtue in his son's choice. Aloysia was young, she had not yet become a great singer and it was too early yet to say if she would mature into a real prima donna. He believed that she had set her mind on the young genius with an eye to the main chance, and that her unscrupulous parents, with so many daughters to provide for, were taking advantage of a boy's infatuation. Wolfgang, with his inability to organise his life, was obviously still a boy though he was in his early twenties, and the Weber parents, if they were not trying to trick him into marriage, should realise his inexperience. Leopold had deliberately spared his son the task of looking after himself so that Wolfgang could devote his time to being a musician, and now that it was necessary for Wolfgang to think practically and sensibly for himself, he could not do so. Leopold, alas, saw no cause to blame himself for the way in which he had brought up his son, and Wolfgang simply accepted his father's wisdom. Like Edmund Gibbon, he 'sighed as a lover but obeyed as a son'. So he set off for Paris with his long-suffering, good-natured, ineffective, ailing mother. When he had made his fortune in Paris, he would return to Aloysia.

Actually, Leopold was wrong about the young singer. No letters dating from Wolfgang's Mannheim and Paris period between the two have survived, and it seems unlikely that she took his ardour very seriously. Ambition, it seems, was her passion, and as Mozart could not at that time further her ambitions she did not take him seriously. His plans to put his genius at the disposal of the girl do not sound like the considered plans of a young man in his twenties—they are more like the daydreams of an adolescent, and once away from her he forgot them. In two years he was writing as devotedly of her sister, Constanze. Aloysia married Joseph Lange, an actor and painter whose unfinished portrait of Mozart, alone among Mozart's portraits, seems to catch his genius (see colour picture on p. 81).

Paris had nothing to offer him that he con-sidered worthy of his gifts. For the Concert Spirituel, the oldest and most aristocratic of Parisian concert organisations, he composed a Sinfonia Concertante for wind instruments (flute, oboe, horn and bassoon, K. App. 9), written for his Mannheim friends, but rivals edged it out of the programme for which it was designed on the excuse that it did not sufficiently consider French taste. The concerto, however, is an expansive, richly scored work, and it handles its solo instruments very resourcefully. For the Duc de Guines, an amateur flautist, and his harp-playing daughter who took composition lessons from him, he wrote a duet concerto, another very objective work made to exploit the instruments in a tasteful way, and in June 1778 he wrote the 'Paris' Symphony (K. 297) for the Concert Spirituel. Because his Mannheim friends were in the orchestra he gave the woodwind and horns more prominence than most composers of the day would have allowed them, and he set out deliberately to appeal to French taste. French audiences liked a work to open startlingly with a display of great unanimity and attack; they set great store by what they called le premier coup d'archet, and the opening of the Paris Symphony was designed to please a taste which its composer thought childish. 'What a fuss the oxen make of this trick!' he wrote to Leopold. 'They all began together, just as they do in other places.' French taste may be responsible too for the work's almost heartless glitter and brilliance, relieved originally by a slow movement, andantino, of great beauty and serenity; it was, however, harmonically too complex, with too great a range of modulation, for its audience. At a second performance on 15 August he gave the symphony a new, pleasant but in no way outstanding slow movement; the symphony has no minuet but its finale is a witty, harmonically surprising movement which works out sonata-form procedures with great polyphonic skill. Writing for a public concert with a large orchestra, Mozart revelled in the presence of clarinets with flutes, oboes, bassoons and two horns as well as trumpets, drums and a string section large enough to balance the brass however loudly they played.

Leopold, of course, was still anxious about his son. A man of strict rectitude and integrity, he could not help Wolfgang, even by exercising his latent talent for intrigue which, despite his incurable high-mindedness and devotion, he was always prepared to employ on behalf of his son. It pained Leopold to be in debt, and in his late fifties he was teaching all hours of the day and enduring a position under a patron whom he disliked no less than did Wolfgang, in order to keep his head above water; and he was beginning to see that although his son was a great musician, Wolfgang would never be able to rescue him financially. The intrigues, jealousies and plots which a rising musician could expect to face were facts of life of which he was clearly aware, and he knew that Wolfgang was ill-equipped to deal with them. Wolfgang's letters were usually lively, amusing, shrewd in their estimates of other people; to please his father he wrote as he had always written, as though without a care in the world and as though the business of surviving and succeeding demanded no special skills. Wolfgang said directly whatever he thought about the music and performances of other musicians, however tactless his opinions might be. If he went to play at a great house, he explained, he did not waste time but took a book to read while other musicians played. He did not flatter in order to make friends or ingratiate himself with other musicians; he accepted praise not as a lubricant to social machinery but as a statement of complete sincerity, and anyone who praised his work was a friend to be trusted for life. It was only too easy to take him in.

The only post offered to Wolfgang was, he reported to his father, that of organist at Versailles. This was a minor appointment which would have given him a great deal of leisure but would have kept him at the palace for six months of every year at a salary of 2000 livres. That, in German money, would have been 915 gulden 45 kreuzer, and life in Paris was expensive, so he was inclined to refuse. Leopold suggested that a less than princely salary for half a year's work would have its compensations in a capital like Paris, giving him ample time for composing other works for the Opéra, the concert societies and for amateurs. Leopold's advice was perfectly reasonable, but Wolfgang refused the post.

Composition, to Wolfgang, was almost always undertaken because music was needed and commissioned. Only when some fresh musical experience provided him with a new area of technique or expression did he write for his own satisfaction; otherwise he would write for patrons or for friends who wanted something to add to their repertoire—horn concertos for Ignaz Leutgeb, clarinet works for Anton Stadler, an oboe concerto for Ferlendis in Salzburg. This meant that any demand was a stimulus. Even the three last of his symphonies, the E flat (K. 543), the G minor (K. 550) and the C major 'Jupiter' (K. 551), were apparently written because the composer was planning a series of subscription concerts at which such works would be needed and not because he wanted, in the 'Jupiter', to say the last word that could ever be said about the reconciliation of polyphonic thought and symphonic style. He would often put off the actual writing down of a work until the last possible moment; his friends were amazed to see him hard at work in the middle of noisy conversations in which he would join from time to time. He could do this because the major work of composition, the creation of melodies, forms and harmonies, was apparently worked out in his head so that comparatively little had to be done on paper; usually the only work he did with a pen in hand was simply recording the music that already existed in his mind. All through his childhood he had worked hard at the music his father had found for him to write. Inde-

Overleaf: The Mozart family painted by Croce in the winter of 1780/81. From left to right: Nannerl, Wolfgang, Anna Maria (portrait) and Leopold.

55

Baron Friedrich Melchior von Grimm, a family friend of the Mozarts and a highly respected member of eighteenth-century Parisian society.

pendent, his father's constant demands silenced, he was happy to procrastinate until the last possible moment.

In Paris, therefore, he composed little; he did not as his father suggested occupy himself with works which could be published and sold to Parisian amateurs to make money. If nobody asked him for music he did not write it—he could be sure, eventually, that commissions would arrive and the quality of his music create the demand that he needed.

Leopold's advice from afar was not heeded; it was good advice for a young musician who had to find ways of earning a few honest pennies. He should choose his pupils carefully rather than court disappointment by offering instruction to all and sundry—who, Leopold asked, would dismiss a satisfactory teacher simply because Wolfgang Mozart was spending a short time in Paris and would be available for a few lessons during his visit?—but he should look for a few amateurs who were already effective players and offer them master classes in interpretation; for such lessons he could justifiably demand a high fee. As for composition, Leopold wrote to his son, 'why, you could make money and gain a great reputation by publishing works for the clavier, string quartets and so forth, symphonies and possibly a collection of melodious French arias with clavier accompaniment.' But this possibility was one which Mozart seemed never seriously to consider. He was convinced that his fate was to become an important *Kapellmeister*, and that other spheres of activity hardly deserved consideration.

On their earlier visit to Paris the Mozarts met Baron Friedrich Melchior von Grimm, a Francophile born in Berlin who had by then lived in Paris for fifteen years, contributed to Diderot's *Encyclopedia* and, in some mysterious way, won great influence in Paris society. In 1764 there had been some social profit in looking after the two little virtuosi from Salzburg, and the Mozarts in their turn helped the Baron to establish himself. But there was little he could do for the adult Mozart, although he did what he could to smooth Wolfgang's way, and wrote a letter of honest if uncomfortable comment to Leopold on 27 July 1778:

> He is too trusting, too inactive, too easy to catch, too little intent on the means that may lead to fortune. To make an impression here one has to be artful, enterprising, daring. To make his fortune, I wish I had but half his talent and twice as much shrewdness ... In a country where so many mediocre and even detestable musicians have made immense fortunes, I very much fear that your son may not be able to make ends meet.

But before Grimm's pessimistic warning had left for Salzburg, Anna Maria Mozart, having dragged herself round Europe in the wake of her son whose sense of what he should do was altogether too insecure and who seemed to gain little guidance from her, quietly died. For a fortnight Wolfgang had nursed her as well as he could. She had missed her family and her Salzburg friends, and was worried by Wolfgang's happy-go-lucky disregard for the practical purposes of their mission. Easy-going herself, she had at last learned Leopold's lesson but could not convey it to her son. Nobody knew what illness brought her death, and on the day she died Wolfgang, not able to bring himself to tell them the truth, wrote to his father and sister warning them of her dangerous illness. By the same post he wrote to a Salzburg friend asking him to break the news.

There was no great sense of direction in Wolfgang's life after the death of his mother. He stayed for about ten days with the Duc de Noailles, who had a private orchestra, and on 8 September a new symphony (apparently a lost second Paris Symphony) was played at the Concert Spirituel. Seemingly admitting defeat and going home to Salzburg without his mother was too painful a prospect to be faced, and it was 26 September before he left Paris and made his way back to Mannheim.

Mannheim had changed. Aloysia and her father had gone to Munich, where Aloysia was now successful enough to need no help from Mozart; according to rumour, her success was in part due to the Elector's more than musical interest in her. But Wolfgang did not hear this until he himself reached Munich, where he wrote to the *Bäsle* asking her to join him and play an important part in some unexplained event there. The people of Salzburg, and especially the Archbishop, would know that he had returned from his tour, and now Wolfgang could find no way of avoiding the humiliation of the Archbishop's service. He returned ripe for rebellion.

The humiliation was avoided through Leopold's gift for negotiation. The post of court organist had been vacant since Adlgasser died, only shortly after Wolfgang left Salzburg. Leopold had originally done nothing about it, but he had come to see that if he could arrange for it to be offered to Wolfgang his son could come home in response to an invitation to a senior post, with his face saved. In the meantime Lolli too had died, and Leopold had unsuccessfully applied for the post of *Kapellmeister* left vacant by his death; Leopold had, however, been given an increase of 100 florins for the extra responsibilities that Lolli's death had brought him. With two senior posts vacant and no outstanding applicant in search of either, Leopold ingeniously arranged that several senior court officials should suggest that an application from Wolfgang for Adlgasser's post would be favourably received, and Leopold for his part suggested that his son would not accept the post at so low a salary as had contented Adlgasser, but finally agreed to the court's terms.

5 The Break with Salzburg

The quarrel between Wolfgang Amadeus Mozart and Archbishop Colloredo inevitably continued. The courts which could not find a vacancy or create a post for the young composer were still capable of distracting him from the Archbishop's service with commissions and invitations, and his patron knew that his new court organist had accepted a post (at three times the salary he had drawn as *Konzertmeister*) but had not sold himself into slavery. When, early in 1781, Wolfgang was commissioned to write an opera for the Elector Carl Theodor in Munich, courtesy made it impossible for the Archbishop to object, and *Idomeneo* came to Mozart as the chance of a temporary escape from a position not unlike imprisonment.

One of his official duties was to teach boys of the cathedral choir school to play keyboard instruments; when a pianist or harpsichordist was needed at court, Mozart played. He composed a Mass (K. 317) in 1779, and another in 1780, as well as the last two of his sonatas for organ and strings played between the Epistle and the Gospel at Mass. There followed three new symphonies for the court orchestra—flutes, oboes, bassoons and strings—which may have reminded him of the brilliance and colour of larger orchestras in Mannheim and Paris. The symphonies are works of great charm, and the second of them, K. 319 in B flat, has a finale of exceptional wit and hilarity, as though the orchestra is working out the denouement of a farcical *opera buffa*, after three movements of unalloyed charm.

The year 1779 also saw the composition of one of the supreme masterpieces, the Sinfonia Concertante for violin and viola (K. 364), rich in melody and deeply moving in its effect of happi-ness shot through with melancholy. Mozart's special affection for the viola—it was his favourite instrument when playing chamber music—is, in a way, a mystery; the instrument had practically no solo repertory and until the twentieth century composers tended to treat it as an unfortunate necessity, singing tenor in the string choir but having no real personality of its own. To Mozart, the viola spoke with a sort of philosophic melancholy.

In 1779, too, came the *Post-horn Serenade* (K. 320). An official serenade for the Salzburg court seems to have been demanded each August, but we do not know its precise occasion. The 1779 work has seven movements, a concertante movement for woodwind soloists and a rondo as well as the two fast movements and two minuets flanking a central slow movement. Haydn wrote serenades and divertimenti making it quite clear that a symphony is a work with higher intellectual qualities than the two lighter forms, but Mozart seems to have regarded the term serenade only as indicating more movements, or a less conventional orchestra, than the symphony. The *Post-horn Serenade* is scored for piccolo and post-horn as well as the standard instruments, and its first movement is worked out with symphonic intensity. Alfred Einstein, the greatest Mozart commentator of the twentieth century and a writer not given to flights of interpretative fancy, sees the first movement as a dramatisation in music of Mozart's dealings with the Archbishop; the violins plead with heartfelt sorrow but are continually interrupted by brusque, peremptory repeti-

An etching by an unknown artist of Archbishop Hieronymous Colloredo, who was to dismiss Mozart from his post as court organist.

61

tions of a single phrase—Mozart pleading for freedom, perhaps, and Colloredo denying it to him. It would have seemed amusing to Mozart to make his patron listen to, and applaud, an unflattering account of their relationship. The post-horn arrives in the second trio of the second minuet as though the persecuted composer (which is how Mozart saw himself) had won his freedom and galloped away into a happier life. It is tempting to think of the post-horn, as restricted in its vocabulary as a bugle, as an obvious symbol.

Even for a composer as prolific as Mozart could be, an opera was not a work to be undertaken without the encouragement of a commission. A composer in service could, perhaps, find time to undertake a simple work purely for his own satisfaction; but his training as a social functionary would discourage him from writing an opera which might never be heard. Nevertheless in the summer of 1779 Mozart set to work on an uncommissioned opera, *Zaide*, in which three Christian prisoners escape from imprisonment in the palace of a sultan. The work was probably encouraged by the fact that the theatre company led by Johann Boehm was occupying the Salzburg theatre; prompted by this, Wolfgang had composed a melodrama (spoken drama with a musical accompaniment), *Semiramide*, the music of which has been lost. The libretto of *Zaide* was based on Voltaire's *Zaire* by Andreas Schachtner, the Salzburg trumpeter, who gave the tragic French original a happy ending (though the work remained incomplete); apparently Schachtner worked so closely with the composer that the libretto goes no further than they had reached when Mozart laid it aside because other, commissioned, work took precedence. The basic plot of *Zaide* returned later as *Die Entführung aus dem Serail*, but *Zaide* is as it stands a more gentle, lyrical work, less brilliant than its successor, and without the furious but fascinating character of

Joseph Quaglio's set of Idomeneo's palace for the original production of Idomeneo *in Munich in 1781.*

Osmin, the keeper of the harem. Mozart's interest in melodrama led him to use accompanied spoken dialogue at times in place of recitative.

Zaide was laid aside because Mozart, who wanted to compose opera, was given the opportunity to write *Idomeneo*. This is heroic *opera seria*; its subject is classical and mythological. It was an immediate success, and Mozart remained in Munich until 12 March, writing some church music and the delightful Quartet for oboe and strings (K. 370). This was a gift for his oboist friend from Mannheim, Friedrich Ramm, a player whom Mozart much admired.

As soon as Wolfgang reached home the Archbishop demanded his presence in Vienna, where Colloredo was on a visit and, apparently, determined to teach the young man a lesson. In Vienna he was part of the Archbishop's personal entourage, living at court in the House of the Teutonic Knights and, he discovered, not allowed to accept invitations from the Viennese aristocracy. He wrote a bitter letter to his father about the company among which he sat at meals—after all, he complained, there were noblemen prepared to invite him to dine at their own tables, while all Colloredo did for him was to prevent him earning money on his own account. Ordered to play at the house of the Russian Ambassador, Prince Galitsin, his instructions were to report early to Colloredo's valet. He deliberately arrived late, and presented himself unceremoniously to the Prince, as though Colloredo had nothing to do with him. The punishment for this public slight was that the Archbishop refused Wolfgang permission to play at the charity concert of the *Tonkünstlersozietät*, an event arranged by Viennese musicians themselves and offering great prestige to those invited to appear. Aristocratic admirers persuaded the Archbishop to change his mind and Mozart's share in the concert was a great success. He decided to capitalise on his presence in Vienna with

The last act of Idomeneo *is set in the Temple of Neptune, here seen in a recent Glyndebourne production.*

a concert of his own to be given in the Burgtheater, but the Archbishop, determined to show egotistical young musicians their place in the scheme of things, forced him to abandon the plan.

Leopold was not in attendance in Vienna, and Wolfgang fulminated by post against his employer. Leopold replied nervously. If the young man were unceremoniously dismissed from service he might find it hard to earn a satisfactory living; so far he had shown no signs of any practical ability which might have made Leopold believe that rebellion could be less than disastrous. It was possible, indeed likely, that rebellion by Wolfgang would have unpleasant results for Leopold himself. At twenty-five Wolfgang was still an obedient, dutiful son; for two months he smothered his rage, though he did point out to his father that if the Archbishop dismissed him or made his life quite intolerable, he would be able, through his musical and social success, to earn his living independently in Vienna as a freelance until an acceptable post came his way. The Archbishop, he said, had cost him 100 ducats through the cancellation of the concert he had planned to give in the theatre. With no more than a couple of pupils he would be better off free in Vienna than in the Archbishop's service. Leopold anxiously warned him against any rashness, drawing from Wolfgang the reply that when the Archbishop ordered a return to Salzburg, he had thought of asking permission to remain behind; out of affection for Leopold, he wrote, he was renouncing 'all his wishes and desires'. 'If it were not for you, I should not hesitate to leave the Archbishop's service. I should give a grand concert, take four pupils, and in a year I should have got on so well in Vienna that I could make at least 1000 thalers.' Obedience to his father's demands for caution, he wrote, was causing him to throw away his chances. Possibilities were opening for him everywhere: he was even promised a contract for a German opera. Either he was a servant who happened to be a musician—which was what Colloredo wanted—or he could abandon the idea of security and live as he wished by his musical wits.

When, on 29 April 1782, a footman ordered the musicians to pack up for their return to Salzburg, Mozart declared that he took his orders from Count Arco, the court chamberlain, and would prepare to leave when he got what he considered to be official orders. On 9 May he was still in Vienna; more orders to move out, delivered by a footman a week before, having been studiously ignored, the Archbishop lost his temper and abused Wolfgang roundly (and to Mozart, unforgivably), ordering him to leave his quarters then and there. He packed up and removed his belongings to Frau Weber's house, where he was given a room. He was followed by a footman bringing a parcel which Mozart was to take to Salzburg with him. He missed the coach and found himself facing another storm from the Archbishop; again he asked for his discharge. Count Arco, who seems to have had some sympathy with Mozart, tried unavailingly to soothe him, but the composer obdurately demanded a reply to his petition for discharge. He wrote to Leopold, reassuring the old man that Count Arco had given his assurance that nothing Wolfgang did would compromise Leopold's position and that Colloredo was so disliked by his equals that the quarrel would do the Mozarts no harm. The first petition for discharge was followed by a second, which was not answered either. When Wolfgang wrote the third, he threatened to deliver it to the Archbishop in person; what he said to the court chamberlain, and how he transgressed court etiquette and protocol, we do not know—the only record of the incident is Wolfgang's own, in which his actions are impeccable—but Arco lost his temper and literally kicked the importunate young man out of the house. Wolfgang was bruised, humiliated, furious and free, regarding the kick in effect as a dismissal.

A painting of Mozart by Lorenz Vogel. This is one of the more obviously romanticised portrayals, bearing little relation to authentic portraits.

6 Constanze

When Leopold, in 1778, was losing patience with Wolfgang's apparent wasting of time in Mannheim and his devotion to Aloysia Weber, the young man defended himself with uncharacteristically priggish self-righteousness. There are people, he wrote, who think that no one can love a girl without having evil designs; but he was a Mozart, a young, clean-minded Mozart, not a seducer like various acquaintances whose names he listed.

Aloysia became an opera star without Mozart's help and promptly, by doing so, opened his eyes to various flaws in her character. She had, he wrote to his father on 9 June 1781, lived on her parents until she could earn, but had married as soon as she gained her position and had done nothing to help her penniless mother.

It was Frau Weber, by this time a widow, who gave Wolfgang lodgings when Count Arco's kick made him homeless. In a very short time he had transferred his devotion to the third of the Weber daughters, Constanze. Just as it had been his duty to lead Aloysia to the top of the tree as a singer, it was now his aim to rescue Constanze from a life of drudgery; she was the one, he explained, who kept house and brought seemliness and order into the life of the Weber family. By 25 July he was explaining to his father that he was the subject of baseless gossip that had him engaged to Constanze simply because he lived in her mother's house. He was not in love with her, but naturally he laughed and joked with her. 'If I had to marry all those with whom I have jested,' he wrote, 'I should have two hundred wives at least.'

In August he moved into rooms in Herr von Aurnhammer's house, 'fit for rats and mice, but not for human beings'. He was teaching the Aurn-hammer daughter, who was useful because she took his father's attention away from the Weber household. His pupil was 'as fat as a farm girl, perspires so much that you feel inclined to vomit and goes about so scantily clad that you really can read as plain as print "pray do look here"'. On 15 December he apparently plucked up courage to tell his father that he intended to marry Constanze. He had not told him before, the letter said, because he could anticipate Leopold's objections to marriage while his income was small and insecure. But physically he needed marriage; his needs were as 'demanding as those of any strong young lover', and he was too religious, too fastidious and had too much care for his health 'to fool about with whores'.

It had to be Constanze. Josefa Weber, the eldest of the sisters, at twenty-three, was lazy, gross and perfidious; Aloysia, false, malicious and a flirt, was by now married and embarked on a successful career; Sophie, the youngest, was fourteen and too young to be anything more than good-natured and feather-brained (eventually, like Aloysia, she became a singer). Constanze, at eighteen, was the kindest, cleverest and best of the bunch. She was responsible for the whole household, a martyr to its needs, not ugly, not beautiful—except for her eyes and a pretty figure. All she wanted was an orderly, organised life.

Actually, Wolfgang broke the news to his father because his hand had been forced. Frau Weber seems to have decided from the start that Mozart would make a husband for one or other of her daughters, and when Aloysia rose in the world Frau Weber set out to disillusion her one-time lover by blackening her character; the stories of Aloysia's meanness were untrue, and Frau

Weber's kindness to Mozart was designed principally to bring him into contact with Constanze, who was more or less compromised by the lodger's friendship. Frau Weber brought along her lawyer, who induced the young composer to sign a declaration that he would either marry Constanze

Previous page: A portrait of Constanze Weber, painted by her brother-in-law Joseph Lange in 1782, the year of her marriage to Mozart.
Above: Mozart's sons, Karl and Wolfgang, aged about fourteen and seven. Of six children born to Constanze, only these two survived. Both were talented musicians, and Wolfgang became a professional.

or pay her an allowance; Constanze herself tore up the document, announcing her entire confidence in Mozart, who considered that both honesty and affection demanded that he should marry her as soon as possible: on the income he received, low as it was, they could manage. On 4 August 1782 they were married, a day before Leopold's reluctant consent reached them. Leopold was more or less reconciled to his son's new life, although it trampled on his dreams; ever since Wolfgang had begun to show his genius as a tiny child Leopold had lived through his son, and it was obviously his hope that a successful, renowned Wolfgang should make a home for his father, who would be secretary, agent, adviser and guide, philosopher and friend to the family genius. The rest of Leopold's life was a grim disappointment. A year after the marriage Wolfgang and Constanze, with their eldest son, visited Salzburg and effected a rather strained friendship between Constanze and both Leopold and Nannerl. They stayed several months but, apparently, were never easy together.

Their first-born child, Raimund Leopold, was short-lived; the second, Karl Thomas, born a year later on 21 September 1784, survived. In 1786 Thomas Leopold was born, and lived for three months; a daughter, Maria Theresa, was born in 1787: she died after six months. A second daughter, Anna, was born and died on 16 November 1789; another son, Franz Xaver Wolfgang, was born on 26 July 1791 and survived. Continual pregnancies weakened Constanze, and in the last years of her husband's life made it necessary to add to the expenses of their shaky household the cost of annual cures. It seems that when Wolfgang claimed that marriage was necessary to him because of the exigencies of his physical appetites he understood himself well.

When Leopold visited the couple in Vienna he told Nannerl that Constance kept house efficiently and economically, feeding her household well—but it may be that a special show was put on to captivate the sour old man.

Constanze had trained as a singer, and if the Incarnatus of the C minor Mass, which Mozart wrote as a thanksgiving for their marriage and which she sang, reflects her voice and abilities she must have been more than promising. When he first became fascinated by Bach fugues, she shared his enthusiasm and implored him to write more fugues.

Constanze was not, perhaps, an ideal wife for Mozart, but he seems to have settled down happily to marriage with her, and to have treated her with a devotion surprising to biographers who notice how near to illiteracy she was and how pained he was, from the time of their engagement, at what he obviously regarded as her flirtatiousness. (He once found her at a party allowing her calves to be measured as a forfeit.)

Wolfgang was a highly sexed man but, at the same time, he was the son of the strictly religious, strait-laced Leopold; the stories of his occasional lapses from devotion to his wife live on without evidence. The fact that he wrote a deeply emotional concert aria with concertante piano accompaniment for Anna Storace has been taken to indicate the depth of his feeling for that obviously delightful young woman, the first Susanna in *Le Nozze di Figaro*. That she was pretty, gifted as a singer and actress, and obviously, in one way or another, fond of him, may easily mean no more than that he was moved by her as he was moved by the texts of his operas. Possibly his devotion to Constanze was intensified by the fact that she gave him grounds for anxiety, real or imaginary. He wondered if she was sufficiently careful of his honour and her own. He never seems to have felt that she cared for him with an intensity equal to his own. His letters to her, towards the end of his life while she was taking the cure and he stayed in Vienna, break out into cries of sexual need so intense that they were obliterated, apparently by Constanze herself.

Something of this sexual intensity is implied in the operas. The fictitious Constanze of *Die Entführung*, threatened with all manner of tortures if she will not yield to the Pasha, sings with ecstatic devotion of Belmonte whom she loves and who, when their plan of escape is thwarted, joins her in an equal ecstasy at the thought of their death together. Then there is Cherubino, the adolescent obsessed by the thought of women and love; the aching sexual jealousies of Count Almaviva and his valet Figaro; Fiordiligi and Dorabella, who care less in reality for the idea of loving a specific individual than simply for loving. Only Don Giovanni does not love; the object of his desire is power. But in *Die Zauberflote* Mozart finds a final statement about love:

> *Mann und Weib, und Weib und Mann,*
> *Reichen zur die Gottheit an.*

Man and wife, individually incomplete, together can reach divinity.

Mozart was an ugly, monkey-faced, unimpressive little man, but as Constanze said, he had a way with him. Aloysia claimed that he had really loved her all his life. Anna Storace destroyed his letters to her, leaving us to wonder. Shortly after Mozart's death a court attache, Franz Hofdehmel, attempted to murder his wife, a pupil of Mozart's, and then committed suicide. The wife was pregnant and gave the son born soon after the names Johann Franz, apparently after Johann Chrysostom Wolfgang Amadeus Mozart and her husband. But despite the unsubstantiated rumours of his lapses, Mozart seems to have been happy with Constanze, remaining devoted, playful and content; his letters are always full of concern for her health and her behaviour, and express his never wearying desire for her.

There seems to be no doubt that fundamentally Constanze was as faithful as her husband. Their marriage was not that of equals, nor indeed could it have been. Perhaps Mozart's equal, in genius and frailty, never existed.

John Brecknock as Belmonte and Valerie Masterson as Constanze in the 1971 English National Opera production of Die Entführung aus dem Serail.

7 Mozartian Economics

Mozart, having at last gained his desired freedom from Colloredo, did not intend to spend the rest of his life as a freelance composer, instrumentalist and teacher. The plan he outlined to his father when Leopold tried to persuade him to avoid a final break with the Archbishop would, he claimed, serve as a stop-gap; eventually the right sort of court appointment would be put at his disposal. The only trouble with Mozart's plans was the same as with all plans made by an optimistic freelance. They depended on his always having an opera commission on hand, on worthwhile pupils and regular, enthusiastically patronised concerts. Delighting in his freedom in Vienna, he could work out his prospects as though they were equivalent to a regular salary, and could think of no obvious reason why such fees and commissions should not be forthcoming.

No position arrived. At the end of 1787 he was appointed court composer to Joseph II. A court composer simply supplied music when it was needed, in exchange for a regular salary—Mozart's pay was 800 gulden a year (see Note on Money, p. 148); for this he supplied only dance music for court balls and masquerades, which must be why his salary was less than half the 2000 gulden a year paid to his predecessor, Gluck. 'Too much for what I have done,' he wrote once on the official receipt for his pay, 'but too little for what I could do.' The death of Joseph II brought him no promotion from the new Emperor, Leopold II. He asked for and was given the job of unpaid assistant *Kapellmeister* at St Stephen's Cathedral, in order to secure the *Kapellmeister*'s post when its holder died. Mozart died first, and on the advice of his friend and patron Baron von Swieten was given a third-class funeral in an unmarked grave to save Constanze, who did not attend, from adding to overwhelming and apparently unpayable debts.

For the last four years of his life Mozart held a court post which made few demands on his time and gave him a salary more than half as large again as that on which his father had kept a family and organised the early concert tours. Not a year passed when Mozart did not earn an appreciable sum from other commissions, from public performances and from playing to the aristocracy. Although his music was controversial, we cannot say simply that he was a genius born before his time, writing for ears and sensibilities too refined

Karl Ditters von Dittersdorf, the composer, who played in the first performance of Mozart's 'Haydn Quartets'.

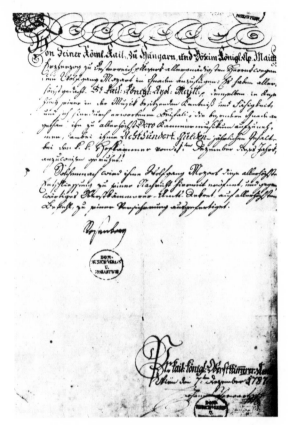

Joseph II's decree appointing Mozart court composer in 1787.

them. He leaves his hearer out of breath.'

Other critics found Mozartian harmony too abstruse and too eager to startle with remarkable dissonances; they accused him of overdressing beautiful and memorable themes with elaborate orchestration in a determination to be original at all costs. Joseph II, a limited but sincere music lover, is said to have told Mozart that *Die Entführung aus dem Serail* was beautiful but had too many notes; the composer's reply was that he had written precisely the correct number. He was said to have put the statue in the orchestra and only its pedestal on the stage. The Emperor complained that Mozart deafened the singers with overfull, heavy orchestrations and he found *Don Giovanni* beautiful but too difficult for Viennese ears.

Such objections do not imply a general rejection of Mozart's music, merely that there were critics who found his music too rich, too lavish with materials and instruments, and too forceful. Those who commented on his brilliance as a keyboard player enthused not only about the grace and delicacy of his playing, but also about its power, forcefulness and eloquence. Actually, such works of his which escaped his control and were free to travel were very widely performed; from *Die Entführung aus dem Serail* in 1784 onwards, his operas travelled swiftly round the German-speaking world, and beyond it to Amsterdam and Paris. *Le Nozze di Figaro* was only three years old when, in 1789, it reached Italy—where Mozart's operas have never been supremely popular. *Die Entführung* was played in thirty-seven towns in less than twenty years; *Le Nozze di Figaro* had twenty-two productions in the same length of time, and *Don Giovanni* nearly seventy. *Così fan Tutte*, a work which did not come into its own until the twentieth century, had twenty productions in its first ten years, and *Die Zauberflöte* was heard in fifty-nine towns before 1800. Mozart's audience stretched throughout Europe to St Petersburg.

A modern opera, enthusiastically received, with

for his own day. Mozart's failure, therefore, demands analysis. If his music was not always popular, it was almost universally interesting: some people doubtless attended performances of his works to enjoy the sense of outrage which has always been one of the pleasures of acknowledging the existence of an avant-garde; in the later piano concertos, for example, old-fashioned listeners must have struggled to assimilate movements which deploy as many as six important themes. Karl Ditters von Dittersdorf, a considerable composer and a friend of Mozart, wrote in his *Autobiography*: 'I have never met a composer who had such an amazing wealth of ideas. I could almost wish that he were not so lavish in using

the aid of modern transport, modern methods of communication, radio, recording and all the adjuncts to popularity of the twentieth century, rarely travels at a comparable speed. But the success of his operas earned Mozart no more than his initial fee. Martin y Soler's *Una Cosa Rara*, first seen in Vienna in 1786, the year of *Le Nozze di Figaro*, was popular and successful (at Don Giovanni's final supper its most popular tune was played by his domestic musicians, to the delight of Leporello); it had twenty-nine productions in Italian, German and Austrian cities, in Paris, Copenhagen, and both Moscow and St Petersburg. This apart, no other late eighteenth-century operas won so much attention as those of Mozart.

A modern composer, legally entitled to performing rights, would earn a considerable amount from such popularity: Mozart and his contemporaries earned an initial fee—normally 100 ducats—for composing and producing an opera. The work then virtually became the property of the theatre for which it was written and from which a score could be obtained by any management wishing to mount a new production. The alterations and adaptations which Mozart made to *Don Giovanni* for its Viennese production in 1788 brought him a second fee of 100 ducats. For the rest, popularity affected his earnings only so far as it created an appetite for further works from him.

Concertos, symphonies and other orchestral works were written for specific occasions. If they were commissioned, they brought him a fee. Most of the piano concertos and the symphonies written after his departure from Salzburg were designed to attract audiences to his subscription concerts or to his concerts in the Burgtheater or outside Vienna; most of them were composed with no commission, and no fee, attached. His violin concertos, like the majority of his church works and his symphonies of the 1770s, were pro-

Mozart plays for Joseph II in the sumptuous surroundings of the court.

ducts of his Salzburg commitments. Works for his friends, such as the Mannheim oboist Ramm, the Salzburg horn-player Leutgeb, and Stadler for whom he wrote the Clarinet Quintet and Concertos, probably earned no money at all. The bulk of his piano sonatas and the sonatas for piano and violin were written in sets of six, on commission, like the three final String Quartets written for the King of Prussia.

Three other sources of income were available to him: the first was teaching, and as we have seen Mozart had little interest in teaching the ordinary run of pupils, wealthy amateurs who would pay reasonably well for lessons from a popular virtuoso like Mozart but whose real interest in music was primarily social. Much of the time he spent rushing by cab from pupil to pupil, he told Leopold, could be spent better on composition, and composition would in the long run prove to be more rewarding than teaching. Mozart was never without pupils, composition pupils rather than instrumental students, but he never built up a lucrative teaching practice among the socially exalted. He was prepared to be enthusiastic about lessons when he was presented with some genuine talent to develop, but he was no good at tolerating dullness or incompetence. Mozart's status in the first years of his Vienna period, when his popularity as a virtuoso pianist was accompanied by great social acclaim, could have secured him as many pupils as he needed or could handle.

Publication was another possible source of income. The development of amateur concert societies and the growth of middle-class amateur solo music-making had created a great demand for printed music of all sorts. During the last half of the eighteenth century, music publishing grew enormously; in print and in manuscript copies music was in demand all over Germany. Not only piano music, solo songs and instrumental pieces (mainly for violin, flute or cello) with piano accompaniment, but also the instrumental parts of orchestral works and chamber music were bought by amateur concert societies, individual

musicians and groups of friends who made music together. Mozart's operas, for example, appeared in piano score with remarkable promptitude after their first performances.

This was a new feature of musical life, which no composer outside Britain and France had learned to organise for his own benefit until Haydn, discovering that French publishers sold large numbers of his works in unauthorised editions issued with not even the slightest reference to himself, decided to issue his works through the Viennese house of Artaria which began to specialise in music in 1776. A publisher issued whatever music came into his hands and was under no compulsion to reimburse or even consult the composer. Haydn sold his works at the best price he could; once they were in print and on sale, the composer had no further rights on them. Publishers made elaborate international tours, collecting potentially profitable works; on one occasion the English publisher John Bland paid for Haydn's String Quartet op. 55, no. 2 with a razor because Haydn at the time was grumbling at the ineffectiveness of the razor he was using.

The system was anything but fair to composers, based as it was on the assumption that a work had been produced to commission and its composer had already been paid by a patron. But Haydn, for example, with his enormous prestige, or any composer who was able or content to follow fashion, could make money and supplement an official income by writing and issuing short, reasonably simple but attractive works that amateurs could play and enjoy; Beethoven, in Vienna without a patron in the years immediately after Mozart's death, when Mozart would still have been no more than forty years old, issued a steady stream of such pot-boilers.

At the end of Mozart's life, however, only a handful—less than a hundred and fifty—of his works had been published, and none of these had been composed specially for publication or sold by him. Leopold's advice to him, to write popular works acceptable to publishers, when his apparently aimless life in Paris was distressing his long-suffering father, was not accepted. It seems that without the stimulus of a commission and the prospect of performance, Wolfgang found it hard to settle to work.

There was obviously less demand for orchestral works, so that in order to make money out of publication—that is, to compose music which amateurs would buy with some enthusiasm—the composer needed to work with publication in view. Music like the succession of concertos which Mozart composed for his own concerts had little appeal to the mediocre pianist playing for his own

Nachricht.

Donnerstag den 10ten März 1785. wird Hr. Kapellmeister Mozart die Ehre haben in dem

k. k. National-Hof-Theater

eine

grosse musikalische Akademie

zu seinem Vortheile

zu geben, wobey er nicht nur ein neues erst verfertigtes Forte piano - Konzert spielen, sondern auch ein besonders grosses Forte piano Pedal beym Phantasieren gebrauchen wird. Die übrigen Stücke wird der grosse Anschlagzettel am Tage selbst zeigen.

Left: A portrait of Mozart by Barbara Krafft, painted after his death.
Above: A notice for a concert given by Mozart in 1785.

pleasure, and he regarded his keyboard works, concertos and solo pieces, as his stock-in-trade as a concert pianist; they could not be released to the world at large until he through his own performance had made them familiar in the concert halls. What eighteenth-century listeners enjoyed was a constant supply of new music in a familiarly conventional style, and if Mozart's concertos and symphonies were in the hands of other pianists and musicians he would need to compose new works for his own use in any concerts he might give outside Vienna as well as those mounted in the city. Therefore he made no real effort to publish his works until he felt sure that familiarity had exhausted their use to him as a concert performer; his determination to keep them out of the hands of rival performers was so great that whenever he was on tour he took with him only the orchestral parts of concertos and played the solo parts from a single sheet of music containing no more than the cues he needed to aid his memory.

When Sebastian Winter, who had been the Mozarts' servant in 1763, became the valet of Prince von Fürstenberg at Donaueschingen, the composer wrote to him on 30 September 1786 to offer the Prince a number of his latest works, with a covering letter explaining his policy:

> The compositions which I keep to myself and a small circle of music lovers (who promise not to let them out of their hands) cannot possibly be known elsewhere as they are not even known in Vienna. And this is the case with the three concertos I have the honour of sending to his Highness.... I must ask His Highness not to let them out of his hands.

During Wolfgang's childhood Leopold sent his juvenilia to publishers, more for the sake of publicity than in the hope of profit; he saw to it that the publisher Immanuel Breitkopf was made aware of the *Wunderkind*'s activities, and it was Leopold who kept in touch with Breitkopf, whom he seems rightly to have regarded as the leading German music publisher. Acting almost ostentati-ously as his son's agent, he wrote to him, on 7 February 1772, immediately after his return from the premiere of *Ascanio in Alba* in Milan, suggesting the range of works his son had available for publication—there were keyboard works, string trios, quartets and symphonies. Three and a half years later, on 6 October 1775, Leopold jogged Breitkopf's memory, reminding him of the music Wolfgang had available but not mentioning the necessity of making any enquiry from the composer himself; all Breitkopf needed to do was let Leopold know what he wanted. In 1781 he tried again, explaining to Breitkopf that Wolfgang had been composing busily and successfully throughout the intervening years, although it may be that all Breitkopf had seen of the result were the six keyboard and violin Sonatas, K. 301–306, which the Paris firm, Sieber, had published in 1778; they were dedicated to the Electress of Bavaria. 'We allow very little to be published,' explained Leopold, underlining the words.

It seems to have been Wolfgang who restricted publication, as though he regarded small, easily available works as unimportant and the big, publishable works as a potential loss of repertoire. Once he had undertaken the complex intellectual task of working out his music and writing down the result, he seems to have lost interest in it except as material for performance; it is possible that his argument that works issued to the public would lose their value as material for concert performance was a mere excuse, a rationalisation of his lack of interest in completed works.

In the 1780s a number of publishers, mainly Viennese, handled music by Mozart, though he came to no arrangement with any one firm. Artaria, Haydn's publisher, paid 100 ducats—equivalent to the fee for a complete opera—for the six string quartets dedicated to Haydn, and published the Piano Concertos K. 413, 414 and 415, the Masonic Cantata *Die Maurerfreude* and the Symphonies K. 319 (originally a three-movement work to which Mozart had added a minuet for performance in Vienna) and K. 385

An unfinished portrait of Mozart by Joseph Lange,
1782.

Leopold Mozart, c. 1765. A portrait by an unknown artist.

*Leopold with Wolfgang and Nannerl, in 1763. A water-
colour by Carmontelle.*

Wolfgang in the gala dress given to him by Maria Theresa.

Above: Die Zauberflöte. *A stage design for the Queen of the Night, by Simon Quaglio, 1793.*

Below: La Clemenza di Tito. *This 1974 Covent Garden production was the first in England since the eighteenth century.*

Left: A scene from the 1955 Glyndebourne production
of Don Giovanni.
Above: Costume design for Papageno by Oskar
Kokoschka for a production of Die Zauberflöte *at the
Salzburg Festival, 1955/56.*
Right: Design for a warrior clad in armour.

Above: Così fan Tutte. *Act I of the 1974 English National Opera production, showing the two heroes taking leave of Fiordiligi and Dorabella.*

Below: Act II of the same production, with Ferrando and Guglielmo disguised as Albanians and Despina as a notary.

(the Haffner), as well as piano and violin pieces to appeal to amateurs. The symphonies and concertos were lost to his repertoire, but chamber music could be released because it had no place in the concert hall. The Haydn Quartets, however, represented Mozart at his most complex and they left a number of listeners baffled; the C major, K. 465 (the 'Dissonance' Quartet), was returned by one subscriber, an Italian, because he believed the strange introduction which gives the work its nickname to be full of engraver's errors, while another tore up the printed parts because they actually annotated the strange harmonies he had heard.

In other words, Mozart did not tailor his music to please a potential audience or soothe the prejudices of his clients; Hoffmeister, another Viennese publisher, instructed Mozart to 'write more popular works, or I shall not be able to publish your compositions'. Criticism of the Haydn Quartets, however, does not mean that they were universally disliked, for very soon after Artaria's publication, Torricella, another Viennese publisher, brought out the six earlier quartets (K. 168–173) composed in Venice more than ten years before, apparently to profit from the musical sensation caused by the Artaria publication and thus creating a good deal of confusion both for himself and for Artaria. He did not intend, he had to explain, to pass these works off as new, and there was no reason to do so because they needed 'no other recommendation than their master's name'.

The success of Mozart's operas meant that each new production created an immediate demand for arrangements to appeal to amateurs; publishers rushed out popular arias, arrangements of selected numbers for string or wind ensembles or for piano, and even complete piano scores. Such arrangements appeared either in print or in manuscript copies. When *Die Entführung aus dem Serail* proved to be a great success, Mozart undertook to produce a piano score for Torricella, but before he had done so, another firm, Lausch, had produced a manuscript piano score. Both Lausch and

Torricella made money from *Le Nozze di Figaro* without any collaboration from the composer. Lausch, again, was first in the field with *Don Giovanni*, and Mozart made nothing from its publication. Both Artaria and Hoffmeister produced vocal scores and various arrangements of *Die Zauberflöte*: again, Mozart was not involved.

We can put into perspective the known condemnations by Mozart's critics when we realise the speed with which such unauthorised arrangements appeared. They were easy to produce and depended on the efforts of badly-paid copyists, who produced not only arrangements but from time to time complete scores. Employed by a composer to produce orchestral and vocal parts for public performances, they could make unauthorised copies and sell them to publishers. Mozart wrote to his father on 15 May 1784 complaining that though the Piano Concertos in B flat (K. 450) and D (K. 451) were in his possession, and those in E flat (K. 449) and G (K. 453) were in no hands but his own and those of the pianist Barbara Ployer, for whom he had written them, copies had somehow leaked out. Haydn, faced with the same piracy, took steps to discover how it had happened and made efforts to prevent it; Mozart seems to have regarded it as inevitable. It was easier to write some more music as soon as a new commission arrived. However precarious his financial position, he made no effort to improve it through a systematic plan of publication. His European reputation—the esteem in which he was held in England, for example, which led him to project a journey there—was largely the result of publications which he had not guided into print but which had certainly profited the publishing pirates. This reputation depended on only one complete opera score, that of *Die Entführung* (the other operas were known from selections), on four symphonies, eight piano concertos, twenty-two pieces of chamber music, piano compositions and songs, most of which were circulated in Europe in pirated copies. Systematic publication could not have made Mozart

rich: it could have provided him, as it provided Haydn, with a steady supplement to whatever other earnings came his way.

The Burgtheater, Vienna, where Mozart gave many concerts.

If Mozart's casual attitude to publication had been based on the importance of keeping his works in his own hands, the reason ceased to be valid by the time he settled permanently in Vienna. Had he committed himself to regular concert tours, his firm grip on his own concert works would have meant that these performances presented the only opportunity for people to hear his music and would have added to the appeal of the concerts. But after 1781 he travelled comparatively little, although giving frequent concerts to the limited audience of Viennese music-lovers, so that he was forced constantly to provide new programmes. Even those Viennese who found his music too abrupt, too irrationally varied in mood, too noisy, too aggressive and too 'learned' wanted to know what he was up to: and he had devoted

supporters. Therefore he was never unemployed, always having on hand commissions of greater or lesser importance or, at least, work to write for a friend. Customs of payment for commissions were strong enough to ensure that, when one was completed, a composer got the agreed fee, the size of which was itself normally a matter of convention. If a composer skimped the work, as Mozart did when he turned the Oboe Concerto K. 314 into a Flute Concerto for the Dutch flautist de Jean, he received less than the agreed payment.

This was a way of earning his living which Mozart understood. In 1784 the Quintet for wind instruments and piano was commissioned by a Polish Count, who paid 180 souverains d'or for the work in advance. Mozart gave a performance of the Quintet before the manuscript was de-

90

livered; having thus broken his contract he offered to refund the money, but the Count would not accept it. The King of Prussia gave 100 Friedrichs d'or for the three 'Prussian' String Quartets (K. 575, 589 and 590). The *Requiem*, which Mozart himself underpriced, was due to bring him 50 ducats on completion.

The musician, Mozart seems to have believed, composed and gave performances: by such activities he earned his living. In 1781 there seemed to be no reason why he should not live a moderately prosperous life on the strength of a few pupils, a number of commissions, a steady flow of publications and frequent performances in the theatre and in the houses of the nobility.

Mozart's concerts in the Burgtheater were important occasions in his and Vienna's musical life. They were given with the professional orchestra which was part of the theatre establishment and with associate artists of distinction. On 23 March 1783, for example, he gave a 'grand concert' in the Burgtheater at which his sister-in-law Aloysia Lange, Therese Teyber and Valentin Adamberger, all three attractive singers from the opera, took part; Mozart played the Piano Concertos in D (K. 175) and C major (K. 415). Therese Teyber sang an aria from *Lucio Silla*, Aloysia an aria from *Idomeneo* and the concert aria 'Mia speranza adorata' (K. 416). Adamberger's contribution was the concert aria 'Misera, dove son' (K. 369), originally composed for soprano. The Haffner Symphony was played. The Emperor attended and listened to the entire programme, which included piano solos and an improvisation. On 22 March another concert at the Burgtheater brought him 1600 gulden, from which, of course, costs had to be deducted. The Emperor, the press noted, was enthusiastic, and Mozart in a letter to his father explained that the Emperor always sent a suitable present to the box office before attending any such concert; had court etiquette been otherwise, the Emperor's pleasure would have led him to give far more. Such events were naturally expensive, and how much Mozart had left when the expenses had been paid is not known. But they added considerably to his prestige, and as he was much in demand at other artists' concerts it seems plain that his appearances were popular.

At the same time he was in great demand to play at the private concerts of the nobility, events which cost him no more than the effort of playing or, quite often, accompanying. Concerts normally took place either on Sundays or in Lent, when the theatre was not occupied with opera. On 3 March 1784 Mozart included a list of his engagements for the month in a letter to his father. Apart from three of his own subscription concerts in the hall of the Trattnerhof, he appeared at three concerts arranged by the pianist Georg Friedrich Richter; he played five times for Prince Galitsin and nine times for Count Johann Esterhazy (he apparently forgot an engagement to play for County Zichy). In addition he planned concerts in the Burgtheater on 21 March and 1 April, but the earlier of the two concerts had to be postponed because most of the best players were engaged to play for Prince Aloys Liechtenstein on that evening. The remuneration from these private concerts was not a fee or a salary but a present, again governed by convention—a prince paid more than a count—but there was no official limit to what an artist might receive if he pleased his patron.

A ticket for one of Mozart's concerts at the Augarten.

*The Graben in Vienna, with the Trattnerhof on the left
(one of the small halls in which Mozart gave concerts).
Inset: the Neuer Markt looking north, with the Mehlgrube (flour mill) on the right. This was turned into a
casino and Mozart often gave concerts there.*

Mozart's own subscription concerts are very poorly documented. As soon as he began to find his feet in Vienna, he became associated with a new venture which he described to his father in a letter of 8 May 1782. Philipp Martin, a Viennese musician, planned a series of twelve subscription concerts in the Pavilion in the Augarten; the subscription was to be two ducats and the orchestra, apart from bassoonists, two trumpeters and drummer, was to consist of amateurs. Mozart estimated that even if expenses were as high as 200 gulden a concert, both he and Martin would have a profit of 200 gulden each. Mozart however took part in only the first of the Augarten concerts (which included one of his symphonies, probably No. 34, K. 338, and the Concerto for two pianos, K. 365). He reported to Leopold on 29 May 1782: 'The first amateur concert went off quite reasonably well. The Archduke Maximilian was there, the Countess Thun, Wallenstein, Baron van Swieten.' Probably Mozart was not simply dropping names but reassuring his father: aristocratic support was the best guarantee of success.

We have little information about Mozart's own first series of concerts in the hall of the Trattnerhof, where he rented an apartment from the end of February 1784. The hall had been converted from a chapel, and for three concerts Mozart paid a rent of 38 florins 54 kreuzer, or nine Austrian ducats. At each concert he played a new piano concerto—the E flat, K. 449, the B flat, K. 450, and the D major, K. 451; the rest of the programmes were not noted. The subscription was 6 gulden, and the copy of the subscription list which Mozart sent to his father on 30 March comprises 172 names. These filled the hall to overflowing. We do not know anything about the composition of the orchestra, how many of its members were professional and how much of the profit it absorbed, but the series seems to have been a success because in the following year Mozart doubled the number of concerts, which now took place at the Mehlgrube, in the Neuer Markt. As Leopold stayed with his son in Vienna from 11 February to 25 April there was no cause for Wolfgang to explain the arrangements, and what we know of the concerts comes from Leopold's letters to Nannerl. The first concert made more than 559 gulden for Mozart; more than 150 people were present, but the rent of the hall cost him half a souverain d'or for each concert. For the first time, it seems, Leopold was able to contemplate his son's future without anxiety: Wolfgang, he wrote, was working extremely hard; several times each week his fortepiano was carried off to a concert. He was paying a high price for the rent of his flat in the Schulerstrasse, but Constanze's housekeeping was economical although the two ate well. Provided that Wolfgang was not in debt to begin with, he should be able to pay 2000 florins into the bank.

Leopold's account of the 1785 subscription concerts was written in mid-February of that year. It notes that the orchestra performed splendidly and that Wolfgang played 'a new and very fine concerto': this was the D minor Concerto (K. 466). On 13 February the soprano Luisa Lasci (who in 1786 was to be the Countess in *Le Nozze di Figaro*) gave a concert in the theatre; Mozart played the Piano Concerto in B flat (K. 456), which he had originally written for the blind pianist Maria Theresa von Paradis to play on her European tour. Leopold found it 'glorious', and said that the 'interplay of instruments brought tears of delight to my eyes'. On the previous evening, Wolfgang had invited Haydn to hear the final three of the six Haydn Quartets: Leopold played the first violin, Wolfgang the viola, and the Barons Anton and Bartholomäus Tinti completed the ensemble. This was the occasion on which Haydn said to Leopold (in the words which the proud father wrote down in his letter of 16 February): 'Before God and as an honest man, I tell you that your son is the greatest composer known to me either in person or by name. He has taste and, what is more, the most pro-

Mozart and Haydn. An unauthenticated anonymous engraving.

round knowledge of composition.'

This was the high-water mark of Wolfgang's success, both social and financial. His rent in the Schulerstrasse was 480 gulden a year—more than he had earned as court organist at Salzburg, not much less than the salary on which Leopold had brought up a family and financed its great international tours. Between 1786 and 1788 Mozart received, as a starting point, sums of 100 ducats for *Le Nozze di Figaro*, and for both the Prague and Vienna productions of *Don Giovanni*. His appointment as court composer to the Emperor in 1787 brought him 800 gulden (although, as previously noted, his predecessor Gluck had been paid 2000 gulden and his successor, Leopold Kozeluch, was to be paid 1500). But in the four winter seasons in which he held the post, all that was demanded of Mozart were thirty-six minuets and the same number of German dances. Whether Joseph II regarded the appointment as a sinecure designed to help an important composer, or felt that Mozart should have a post because of his reputation, we do not know. Joseph II made little use of Mozart, and the composer's unwillingness to compose except to definite commissions prevented his making full use of the subsidy. Nevertheless, 800 gulden was more than Leopold Mozart, and the majority of composers, ever earned; it was pitifully low pay, but it was enough to live on. In 1774, as *Kapellmeister* to Prince Nikolaus Esterhazy, Haydn's pay was only 400 gulden a year with the emoluments which went with residence in the palace.

It is still impossible to explain fully why Mozart ended his life in ruin. *Le Nozze di Figaro* was so overwhelming a success that the Emperor had to forbid encores; the one-act *Der Schauspieldirektor* brought him 50 ducats. He revised *Idomeneo* (turning Idamante from a castrato role into a normal tenor part) for Prince Auersperg. In April 1786 he gave a concert in the Burgtheater (Abert, the great pioneer of Mozart biography, described this as the first of three concerts, but there is no record of the other events), at which the C minor Piano Concerto had its first performance. In 1787 he gave a concert for Count Thun, and after the triumph of *Le Nozze di Figaro* in Prague gave a concert there at which the 'Prague' Symphony was performed. There do not seem to have been any major public concerts in Vienna in 1787, but the demand for his work at private concerts did not abate. His small-scale Sunday morning concerts were the only concerts of his own that he gave during the rest of his life.

Don Giovanni triumphed in Prague in 1787 and, despite criticism, was acclaimed in Vienna a year later, but it could not recompense him for the fees which he seems no longer to have commanded as a virtuoso. He projected a series of subscription concerts in 1788, but the prospectus he circulated came back with the name of only one subscriber—it was that of Baron van Swieten, an ex-diplomat and a lover of the music of Bach and Handel; he had served in the Embassy in London and had learned Handel's music there. He gave concerts on Sunday mornings, and not having an organ in his home, paid Mozart to rescore the Handel oratorios, replacing the continuo organ in adaptations which show us the early eighteenth century through the eyes of a later generation.

For Mozart the situation was gloomy enough to produce moods of hopeless melancholy. Apparently he was incapable of any rational economies, and his wife's continual pregnancies had damaged her health so that the cost of cures away from home had to be added to their expenses. The situation was beginning to slide beyond his control, but he thought only of the money he could make if he could reach England, and asked his father to take charge of his two small sons in Salzburg while he and Constanze crossed the channel; Leopold wrote forcefully, harshly but sensibly to point out the absurdity of expecting an old man to look after two infants, and Wolfgang made no effort to work out an

Antonio Salieri, court composer during the years Mozart spent in Vienna.

96

alternative plan. In the following year, on 28 May 1787, Leopold died.

It was Mozart the concert pianist rather than Mozart the composer whose reputation had slumped. His operas continued to be performed all over Germany, and those of his compositions which were available were played in concert programmes. It may simply have been that Mozart, having been heard repeatedly at public and private concerts in Vienna since 1781, had played too much and too often to keep the attention of an audience which did not consist entirely of dedicated music-lovers; many of those who had begun by idolising Mozart had done so because he was a fashionable success—when the fashion changed, their support evaporated.

It seems likely that Mozart's personality added to his difficulties. He was friendly, good company, lively, witty and charming. But he judged the playing and the compositions of his contemporaries with merciless severity. As a matter of course, he was the rival of every composer competing for the attention of any available audience, and he dismissed out of hand the whole range of contemporary music apart from that of Haydn. Even composers like Gluck, who had made considerable efforts to assist him, discovered that his attitude to them was mockery and derision. Told that Mozart had been speaking against him, Haydn found the information easy to believe. 'I forgive him', said the older master, but most of Mozart's rivals were less understanding. There were those who idolised him and were conquered by his liveliness and charm; but they were not composers. The young man who had taken a book to read while others entertained the audience at a musical party had learned neither tolerance nor tact.

He came across the music of Vincenzo Righini in Vienna in 1781 and explained to his father, in a letter of 29 August, that Righini composed charmingly but was a monstrous thief. Telling him of the piano-playing competition in which he claimed he had defeated Clementi (who actually advanced piano technique in directions Mozart would not follow), he declared that his rival was a good keyboard technician, but 'apart from that he has not a farthing's worth of taste or feeling; he is a mere *mechanicus*'. Part of the competition was that Mozart and Clementi should play in turn alternate movements of a sonata by Paisiello; these, he declared, were wretchedly written. The various schemes of Antonio Salieri, the Emperor's *Kapellmeister*, to prevent Mozart's appointment to the Emperor's musical staff are explained in his letters to his father. But in December 1783 he dismissed Salieri's German opera, *Der Rauchfangkehrer*, as a wretched work. Sociable and talkative as he was, he talked as he composed, and his tongue earned him the enmity of musicians who might, had he been less given to derision and rejection, have been his devoted supporters.

His impracticality, which may have been the result of an upbringing in which Leopold undertook to deal with all practical matters, left him incapable of finding solutions when life presented him with problems. He rapidly realised that the success of *Die Entführung aus dem Serail* did little for him but made theatre managements rich. 'I am willing to write an opera,' he wrote to his father on 5 October 1782, 'but not to look on with 100 ducats in my pocket and see the theatre make four times as much in a fortnight. I intend to produce my operas at my own expense; I shall clear 200 ducats for those performances and then the theatre may have it for fifty ducats.' The rewards Mozart (or for that matter any composer) received for his work were anything but fair, and if he had been able to keep control of his operas he would have made enough money to transform his life.

But the scheme has no contact with reality. Even where there were theatres available for his use, Mozart must have been aware of the expenses of mounting an opera. The cost was already so high that even in Vienna the national opera had been handed over to the villainous Affligio who had prevented the child Mozart's first opera from reaching its stage. The plan for the tour of England was more feasible, but for all the keenness

with which Mozart talked of it, its dependence on
his old father's willingness to look after the small
children removed it from the realms of practi-
cality, and the composer attempted no other less
improbable scheme.

By 1787 Mozart had become miserably conscious of failure. He had not won the sort of position and security to which he felt his gifts entitled
him, and he knew full well the quality of his own
work. His situation became desperate not only
because he was, or felt himself to be, defeated by
a harsh destiny but because through his impracticality he lost the will to cope with his difficulties.

Mozart's improvidence, his habit of spending
whatever money came his way, his wife's constant
pregnancies, made financial stability impossible.
There was no Leopold to tell him what to do, and

*Muzio Clementi, composer and piano virtuoso, who met
Mozart in a piano-playing contest before Joseph II.*

Constanze, who later handled his manuscripts
with considerable shrewdness, seems at that stage
to have been completely governed by his easy-
going attitude. The tragedy is not that of an innocent crushed by a hostile world: it is, as already
noted, the classical tragedy of a supremely gifted
hero destroyed by the weakness of his character.
But even that weakness became musical profit;
the special beauty of Mozart's later works—the
Clarinet Concerto and the final Piano Concerto,
for instance—is their amazing ambivalence of
emotional statement. Triumph, disaster, glory
and sorrow, gaiety, joy and terror exist together
in one total experience. Mozart presents not
emotion but life.

99

8 The Dramatist

Mozart was eight years old when he first said that he wanted to compose an opera and twelve when he had his first opportunity to do so; at twenty-three, after nine other apprentice works, he wrote *Idomeneo*, his first stage masterpiece. Three un-commissioned operas—one German and two Italian—left incomplete show his dedication to opera. Mozart wrote masterpieces in every form he touched, but opera is the essential key to his work; it associates his music with personalities and events, and with the emotions generated by these. The themes and their treatment in the operas are often recalled and explained in his instrumental works.

The Oboe Concerto (K. 314) written in 1777 for the Salzburg first oboist, Giuseppe Ferlendis, ends with a rondo the theme of which to all intents and purposes returns as the aria 'Welche Wonne, welche Lust', in *Die Entführung aus dem Serail*, in which the English girl, Blonde, looks forward to the prospect of escape and freedom. Whether Mozart, in 1782, consciously looked back to a theme he had written five years before and decided that it was appropriate to the idea of freedom and its joys, or whether he simply recomposed the rondo theme without remembering that he had used it before is a pointless speculation, but as like causes bring about like results, we recognise that the concerto and the aria explore and express similar varieties of delight.

Innumerable similar instances occur. Perhaps the most fascinating of the personalities created in *Die Entführung* is Osmin, the violent, blood-thirsty but ineffectual guardian of the harem: the other characters in the work represent heroism, fidelity, magnanimity and so on, but Osmin succeeds in existing simply as a personality—which

may have been the reason Mozart returned to the character in the Haffner Symphony three months after the opera's production. But the Symphony presents a new aspect of Osmin's personality, showing him in circumstances happier than those which constrained him in the opera.

There are few bars in music more delicious than those in the second act of *Le Nozze di Figaro*, in which Count Almaviva, suspecting his Countess of misbehaviour with the page-boy Cherubino, is about to break open the door to her room when it opens of its own accord and he is confronted not by evidence of her guilt but by her maid, Susanna. The strings play the demurest of themes over which Susanna addresses her master in phrases of the most knowing innocence, entirely deflating his rage and a dangerous situation. This situation is more or less reproduced in the Piano Concerto in E flat (K. 482), actually completed three months before the opera's production. In the Concerto, however, the Count is not reduced to baffled silence; he argues and defends himself powerfully, as though here Mozart is working out an alternative denouement to the situation which, on the stage, the Count cannot handle.

Oddly enough it is often in the operas that alternative resolutions are presented to situations originally conceived, so to speak, in concert works. The slow movement of the Piano Concerto in E flat, K. 271 (the first completely mature piano concerto Mozart wrote, composed in 1777, nine years before *Le Nozze di Figaro*), comes from the same area of experience as that in which Barbarina, the adolescent daughter of Count Almaviva's gardener, finds life too complicated to be mastered. The finale of the same concerto seems also to foresee the phrase with which Monostatos,

Above: The final scene from an 1854 production of Die Entführung aus dem Serail. *The opera was first performed in Vienna in 1782, and was Mozart's first great success.*

Below: The same scene from the 1971 English National Opera production, with Alexander Young as Belmonte, Lois McDonall as Constanze, and Richard Van Allen as Osmin.

the evil negro of *Die Zauberflöte*, explains that even negros suffer the pangs of love; the concerto was written fourteen years before *Die Zauberflöte*. The duet of Susanna and Cherubino, 'Aprite, presto aprite', in Act Two of *Le Nozze di Figaro* (in which Susanna persuades Cherubino to save himself from the angry Count by leaping from the Countess's window) is echoed by the finale of the Prague Symphony, K. 504. The symphony was composed a year after the opera, and it has both unexpected suggestions of the Masonic solemnities of *Die Zauberflöte* and anticipations of the divine vengeance which a year later was to chill the blood in *Don Giovanni*, which Mozart did not know, when he first visited Prague, was to be his next opera. It is impossible to say to what extent the composer was consciously employed in thinking out dramatic situations in music, although Mozart's complete intellectual control of all his music makes it seem likely that he was aware of its dramatic foundations at points of great emotional intensity.

At the same time the Mozartian affinity between sonata form and drama led him to use sonata form as the means by which the music itself should embody stage action; individual arias and ensembles are deployed in sonata form not merely as a method appropriate to drama, but as a means of actually creating the dramatic situation in music.

Mozart's position as the supreme musical dramatist rests, first, on his power to create music for specific characters. Characterisation is perhaps the fundamental dramatic quality, but action, which Mozart creates symphonically, is a particular feature of his operas. More than any other composer he creates in music the actual rhythms and pace of action. His predecessors, like Gluck, had spent a decade or more breaking away from the constraints of *opera seria*, but the real operatic reform came through Mozart's recognition of the intrinsically dramatic quality of the symphonic idea.

In Act One of *Le Nozze di Figaro* Susanna, who is to marry Figaro, is the target of Count Almaviva's current desires. For the sake of popularity the Count has renounced his rights to the *ius primae noctis*, the tradition which gave him the right sexually to initiate any unmarried woman on his estate and in the past would have given him such a right over Susanna. Count Almaviva's palace also houses Cherubino, a page-boy (and therefore an aristocrat) just old enough to be fascinated by young women; Cherubino idealises the Countess but is prepared to pay attention to all the young women of the staff, and he calls on Susanna partly to flirt, partly to discuss the Countess. When the Count arrives to attempt to win Susanna over, Cherubino hides because he is already in disgrace with his master. They are interrupted by Don Basilio, the cleric who is the Countess's music-master, a man fascinated by gossip and slander, and so the Count hides. Don Basilio attempts to further the Count's cause with Susanna, but does so in terms which provoke the Count into revealing himself and declaring that Cherubino shall be banished from court and found a commission in the Count's regiment. This is the beginning of a trio (Cherubino remains in hiding), 'Cosa sento'. The sentence of banishment is a firm, remorseless first subject, and both Basilio and Susanna provide second subjects in the technically correct key. Basilio's thematic contribution is a single suave phrase, Susanna's an agitated passage which opens up the harmony and allows considerable harmonic movement: the agitation of Susanna and the remorselessness of the Count are thus created in purely musical terms. When the Count explains Cherubino's latest prank—he was caught only the day before in very compromising circumstances with the gardener's young daughter, Barbarina (he tells this story in the second-subject melody first provided by Don Basilio)—he discovers Cherubino's

Geraint Evans as Figaro and Reri Grist as Susanna in Act I of the 1971 production of Le Nozze di Figaro, *at the Royal Opera House, Covent Garden. Susanna is admiring herself as she tries on her wedding veil.*

hiding place; the sonata-form trio thus reaches its recapitulation, with the Count's angry determination to be rid of Cherubino restated, given greater dramatic force by what has been enacted in the music itself.

Because, in Mozart's day, the most fruitful intellectual discipline to which a composer could

Le Nozze di Figaro. *At the end of Act I, Cherubino is banished from court.*

aspire was that of sonata form, Mozart's principle of symphonic opera created stage music not only with real dramatic power but also with great intellectual strength. The multiplicity of events and actions which it is possible to embody in terms of exposition, development and recapitulation— a brief allusion to a new key, reference to a key visited and left, or even a change of orchestral colour can be counted as events—enabled Mozart to create actual drama in musical terms. The trio in Act One of *Le Nozze di Figaro* is a movement in B flat major; the second subjects of Basilio and Susanna both rightly plead with the Count in F major, the dominant; the Count refuses in E flat, the key of the subdominant, as though Mozart were employing one of Haydn's favourite devices and announcing a false recapitulation in a key that will again have to be abandoned. Thus the suspense is heightened until the Count repeats his final, definitive ruling in B flat.

Mozart's determination to find a more fully dramatic style of opera, music not restricted simply to a commentary on the emotional re-actions of the characters but actually composing the events and actions themselves, demanded a new and more inclusive time scheme for the work. Mozart's symphonically orientated movements allow him the time he needs to compose the action. Miraculous as are, for example, the Countess's two arias in *Le Nozze di Figaro*, 'Porgi amor' and 'Dove sono', the supreme miracles of Mozartian opera are the big ensembles and act finales, in which several personalities interact and express their individual responses to every situation while faithfully maintaining their characterisation in music of complete coherence and integrity.

The second-act finale of *Le Nozze di Figaro* is an intricate comic imbroglio in which Figaro and Susanna plot to thwart the Count's exercise of his privilege; the Countess plots to shame him into fidelity; and Marcellina the housekeeper and her lawyer Dr Bartolo plot to extort heavy damages from Figaro, who has promised to marry Marcellina in return for a loan or to compensate her with money if he fails to do so. Don Basilio joins in as a delighted mischief-maker. Another peripheral character, a stupid, drunken gardener, is drawn into the situation to add to its complexity. The twists and turns of deception and the uncertain fortunes of the combatants are totally realised in music in which each participant remains true to his own tone of voice—the Count's arrogance, Figaro's impudent habit of taking up the Count's themes and using them for his own purposes, the Countess's longing for a renewal of the love between her and her husband, and even the gardener's stupidity are featured in an uninterrupted stretch of music in several movements. The music is not expressed in the form of first and second subject, but the symphonic style of development provides its motivating power and also its splendid wit. The finale begins as a duet in E flat, marked *allegro*; the Count is determined to find and punish Cherubino for his presence in the Countess's room; the entry of Susanna and the discomfiture of the Count take the music into B flat and the tempo to *molto andante*; it hurries into an *allegro* in which the Count is forced to apologise for his unjust suspicions. A modulation to G major opens an *allegro* in which Figaro arrives with problems of his own to settle— he has sent the Count an anonymous letter warning him that while he is hunting his wife will entertain a visitor. Then, in F major, at *allegro molto*, the gardener arrives to complain about the damage to the garden done by the man who jumped from the Countess's window, dropping a document on the way. The man was the terrified page and the document his hasty, unsealed commission. Figaro admits responsibility for the damaged flowers and the document and, with the help of the Countess and Susanna, contrives an explanation. The forces now involved have become a quintet, and the departure of the gardener relaxes the movement to *andante* and the key to B flat, safely on the way to a conclusion tightened up to *allegro assai* and now home in E flat, with Marcellina, Basilio and Bartolo arriving to demand a settlement of Marcellina's case against Figaro. E flat, of course, tells us that the side-issues may have been resolved key by key, but that the essential problem of Figaro's

freedom to marry Susanna remains unsolved. Each section of the growing finale adds a new participant and a new problem worked out by the development of its own theme, so that the entire situation is realised in music.

The special feature of *Le Nozze di Figaro* is the way in which it creates the world and society of eighteenth-century Europe. The idea of a libretto based on Beaumarchais's politically objectionable play was, apparently, Mozart's. His librettist, the Italian-Jewish Lorenzo da Ponte, had the task of assuring the Emperor that only the comedy would remain in the libretto and that its politically dangerous view of society would be omitted. Nevertheless, although da Ponte omitted from the

Left: Le Nozze di Figaro, *Act IV. Susanna, disguised as the Countess, drives Figaro from the garden.*
Below: The garden scene in the same act of the 1971 Covent Garden production.

last act of the play a soliloquy in which Figaro expressed his furious hatred of the old régime and its privileges, the political danger of the opera persists. Figaro and Susanna, a valet and a maid, foil the plan of their aristocratic patron, who is not only forced to abandon his pursuit of Susanna but is also shamed into a promise of fidelity to his wife. English audiences do not always notice refinements of expression in Italian, and it should mean more to the listener than it often does that Figaro refers to his employer as 'Signor Contino' ('Little Mr Count') and that his splendid aria 'Non piu andrai' not only mocks the military pretensions of the nobility but also addresses Cherubino, for all the superiority of the boy's birth, in the familiar and patronising second person singular. The opera remains revolutionary because not only is it the story of how a valet and a maidservant prove to be superior to the Count in intelligence and

moral attitudes; they are conscious of their superiority and dare to proclaim it.

The world of *Le Nozze di Figaro* is inhabited by men and women who exist as personalities, not merely as representatives of emotion or social status. The Countess's love for her faithless husband, like Figaro's fierce sexual jealousy, transcends the stereotyped psychology on which baroque opera had almost totally depended. The people of *Le Nozze di Figaro* are individuals living in a society as comprehensible to us and as imperfect as any other. Its wit is not simply in words: as the opera opens, Figaro is measuring the room allotted to him and his wife-to-be to make sure where the bed would fit most conveniently. He praises the consideration of the Count in arranging that their bedroom should be so near to the rooms of the Count and Countess; suppose, he says, that the Countess wants Susanna early in the morning—a few paces and she reaches her mistress. Susanna has some doubts; suppose the Count sends Figaro early in the morning with an important message—a few paces and the Count is with her. The bell which calls Susanna to her mistress is a nice gentle tinkling; that which sends Figaro off on his hypothetical message is the loud braying of a horn, which is not simply an incongruous and therefore amusing effect but a pun reminding us that the horn is the symbol of cuckoldry.

The early operas, from *La Finta Semplice* to *Il Rè Pastore*, have passages of great beauty. They show the young Mozart exploring operatic conventions and working with the greatest tact in close contact with singers from whose experience and expertise he must have profited. But in the early operas through which he learned his art it is the ensembles which lead him to understand and individualise his characters. Their personalities are portrayed through their interaction with each other. In them, Mozart teaches himself to master the various conventions and to charge conventional ideas with powerful individuality. The operas for Milan, and those which closely succeeded them, show him developing the sense of drama which was to revolutionise opera, but even the orchestration of these early operas is kept down within conventional limits. When he was denied any regular theatre work in Salzburg and set to work on *Zaide* simply to satisfy a personal ambition, he charged it with beautiful music, and though it has less variety of incident and character than the same situation in *Die Entführung aus dem Serail* what remains of the work has sufficient character and vitality to leave a listener sad that it was never completed. *Zaide* was Mozart's first fully ambitious attempt to deal with a German text. He wrote to his father at length and with considerable force on the desirability of German opera, as though through *Zaide* he was moving into an area of expression which he was eager to cultivate perhaps simply because, at that time and with a touring company visiting Salzburg, German opera had a greater chance of production than an Italian work would have had. Mozart obviously preferred the work actually in hand to theoretical work which he might have attempted under other circumstances; it never seemed other than natural to him that there should be German opera, although he realised that the difference of language would involve differences of style and approach.

The demand for *Idomeneo* ended his work on *Zaide*, and *Idomeneo*, composed for fine singers in a great theatre with a first-rate orchestra, made quite distinct demands on him. The music of the opera for Munich is specially remarkable in the richness of its colour as well as in its inexhaustible lyrical appeal and the way in which the composer totally identified himself with the stage personalities. For the first time Mozart was forced to think out the dramatic implications of the legend with which he had to deal and to realise them in music. The tale is that of King Idomeneus of Crete, who returning from the Trojan War and prevented by sea storms from reaching his home, rashly vows a sacrifice to Neptune in return for his safety—the life of the first Cretan he should meet. The victim, accidentally encountered, is his son Idamante. The situation is capable of great emotional intensity, but it is developed in several directions. Idamante himself is guarding Ilia, a Trojan hostage who is in love with him and with whom he is in love. Electra, the daughter of the murdered Agamemnon, has taken refuge in Crete since she has been party to the killing of her mother; she too loves Idamante. She is a passionate, vengeful woman, while Ilia is gentle and submissive, so that Mozart has two kinds of love to occupy him. The patriotic counsellor Arbace offers yet another area of intensity. Idomeneo's attempts to cheat the god Neptune, Idamante's killing of the sea monster sent to ravage Crete and his willingness to die for his father's vow bring supernatural horror and simple heroism into the score, and the resolution of its problems demands a new solemnity. Mozart luxuriated in the work's opportunities.

Idomeneo was a Salzburg collaboration. Its librettist was the Abbate Varesco, the Archbishop's court chaplain, a man with some local reputation as a poet but not an experienced librettist. At the beginning of November 1780 Mozart went to Munich to work with the singers and from then on bombarded his father by post with comments and suggestions, and with commands and demands, to pass on to Varesco. The libretto was based on a French opera set to music in 1712, and Varesco attempted to convert it into the sort of libretto that Metastasio might have constructed, in strict obedience to the principles of traditional *opera seria*. But Mozart thought otherwise. The arias he wanted were not the conventional da capo arias which kept the action restricted to recitatives; more in the style of French opera than *opera seria*, Mozart integrated the chorus into the action instead of leaving it simply to comment on events. The beauty and elaboration of the orchestration could easily have been the cause of Joseph II's later objections to the lavishness of detail with which Mozart was supposed to damage singers' voices. *Idomeneo*

refuses under any circumstances to be conventional *opera seria*, but suggests that the composer was attempting a reconciliation of French and Italian styles in the interests of drama.

'In opera', Mozart wrote in one of the letters meant to teach Varesco his business as a librettist, 'poetry must be the obedient servant of the music.' One can feel sorry for the unfortunate Abbate under the relentless tyranny of his collaborator. Nothing that could be conveyed by music was to be elaborated in words. Mozart's demands for brevity and simplification insist over and over again on the excision of lines which Varesco valued for their poetic quality, and if these demands were not immediately met Mozart proved capable of making whatever rearrangements and compressions he felt to be necessary. Varesco felt, for example, that Electra could not simply disappear out of the work without her future settled; she should marry somebody. Perhaps she should marry Idomeneo himself. But Mozart wanted to do no more than was essential to the drama and took no interest in glib, arbitrary solutions offered without dramatic justification.

The idea that Mozart set to work on *Idomeneo* as a conventional *opera seria*, unwillingly hampering himself with a form he already knew to be outdated, does not tally with the unorthodox dramatic strength of the work as he composed it, paring away everything in text and musical convention which could not be justified as drama. *Die Entführung aus dem Serail* has been criticised on less dubious grounds. It was the immediate result of Joseph II's policy for the Viennese state theatres. In 1776 the Emperor had put an end to the practice of farming the theatres out to a commercial management expected to run them at a profit. For motives partly patriotic and partly financial the Emperor had set out to establish German opera, and two years later had disbanded the Italian opera and ballet companies and set up a German company, the National Singspiel, in their place. The members of the new company consisted of actors rather than singers, and their repertoire depended chiefly on translations from French and Italian works. The development of a company of Germans who were definitely opera singers demonstrated the need for genuine operas in the German language. North German *Singspiel*, already a popular form, did not appeal strongly in Italianate Vienna, and Mozart was already awaiting his opportunity with a German translation of *Idomeneo* and the incomplete *Zaide*.

Die Entführung aus dem Serail differs from *Zaide* principally in the greater richness and emotional range of its libretto, the work of a distinguished and thoughtful dramatist known as Stephanie the Younger, to distinguish him from his elder brother. The story of European girls—a maid and her mistress—in Turkish hands and rescued by their lovers, servant and master, had been in existence for almost half a century. It seems to have begun with Dryden's play *Don Sebastian*, which had been transformed into an English ballad opera, *The Captive*. The forerunner of Stephanie's libretto was a play by one Bretzner, *Belmonte und Constanze*; Bretzner was highly indignant at the treatment his work had received from its adaptor, who was dominated by Mozart as Varesco had been. Apart from demands for alterations when the words seemed to have little sympathy with a musical setting, Mozart sent precise instructions for the way in which passages should be rewritten and for the rhythms he required. Deciding that Osmin needed another aria, Mozart sent its music to Stephanie to be fitted out with words. As he was this time in close contact with his librettist, Mozart's letters to his father deal not with practical details of composition but with his aims and with the dramatic principles the work must embody.

Singspiel permitted spoken dialogue and reserved its music for scenes of emotional intensity; it made little use either of ensembles or of the chorus. It had developed in the commercial theatres of north Germany, appealing to a popular audience and resembling English ballad opera rather than developing any specifically German style. Working for Joseph II's company and aiming at a more ambitious style musically, Mozart so to speak Italianised the music, tending to set every number for its own sake rather than as a component part of a single design. The two lovers, Belmonte and Constanze, exist through splendidly ardent, youthfully idealistic melody. They are balanced by their more down-to-earth servants. Osmin, angry, but gullible and too silly to be really dangerous, opposes the quartet of lovers. The problem here, to Mozart, was one of aesthetics. How did a composer deal with a character whose nature 'oversteps all the bounds of moderation and propriety', Mozart asked his father. The question was purely rhetorical.

> As passions, whether violent or not, must never be expressed in such a way as to excite disgust, and as music, even in the most terrible situations, must never offend the ear but must please the hearer, or in other words must never cease to be music, I have gone from F (the key in which the aria is written) not into a remote key, but into a related one, not, however, its nearest relative, D minor, but into the more remote A major.

Mozart did not often write about his expressive intentions, but his letters about *Die Entführung* show him doing so. Belmonte's aria, 'O wie ängstlich, O wie feurig', has an accompaniment which conveys Belmonte's loving heart. 'You feel the trembling—the fluttering—you see how his throbbing breast begins to swell.' He was delighted, too, by the opportunity to use 'Turkish music'—bass drum, triangle and cymbals (which he had splendidly evoked in the 'Turkish rondo' finale of his A major Piano Sonata, K. 331)—and by the rowdy Janissaries' chorus in praise of the Pasha, a speaking character whose generous humanity provides a happy ending for the lovers.

It was an apt coincidence that gave Mozart a heroine named Constanze to make adorable at a time when his own life was centred on a Constanze, and no music embodies more perfectly an ardent, youthful love. Every aspect of the music

Neues Singspiel.

Die Kaiserl. Königl. National - Hof - Schauspieler
werden heute Dienstag den 16 July 1782 aufführen:

(Zum erstenmal)

Die Entführung aus dem Serail.

Ein Singspiel in drey Aufzügen,
nach Breznern frey bearbeitet und für das k. k. Nationalhoftheater eingerichtet.

In Musik gesetzt vom Herrn Kapellmeister Mozart.
Die Bücher sind beym Logenmeister für 17. kr. zu haben,

Der Anfang ist um halb 7 Uhr.

is vivid and beautiful—from Pedrillo, the servant,
preaching courage while trembling with fright,
and the pert comicality of Blonde, to Osmin's
murderous rages and Constanze's heroic defiance.
Every number in the opera is rich and expressive,
though its German framework gives it a looser
structure than the total coherence of *Le Nozze di
Figaro* and *Così fan Tutte*. In his other operas
Mozart studied the conventions and carefully
worked out the points at which he expanded or
abandoned them; it was not that he needed a convention to direct his footsteps but that the existence of one enabled him to find his own way with

Above: A play-bill announcing the first production of
Die Entführung aus dem Serail *at the Burgtheater,
Vienna, on 16 July 1782.*
Right: Ludwig Fischer, the first Osmin in Die Entfüh-
rung aus dem Serail.

greater clarity. *Die Entführung* is a more loosely constructed score of ardent vitality, perhaps over-indulgent to its star singers: Mozart said that he had made sacrifices to what he called 'the flexible throat' of the first Constanze, Madame Cavalieri. Threatened with torture if she will not submit to the Pasha, Constanze launches into a gorgeous concert aria, a rondo, with obligato flute, oboe, violin and cello; this is a marvellous opportunity for a great coloratura soprano, but it grows out of scale with the action and its tempo, leaving the Pasha with nothing to do except listen to a concert. Loosely constructed though the opera is, the quality of the music, granted accurate and spirited performance, delights, moves and charms.

Wagner, writing in the 1850s, accused Mozart of a failure to work out a consistent theory of opera, and of acting like any other dutiful court composer in accepting any libretto handed to him. Though we can find no complete theory of the relation of music to libretto, his letters and his practice as a composer imply standards and theories which were entirely practical and realistic. Wagner's essentially epic view of the theatre insisted that characters should be representative figures personifying superhuman qualities. Mozart on the other hand created characters capable of weakness and inconsistency. *Le Nozze di Figaro*, for example, quickly demonstrates the daring and resourcefulness of Susanna's mind; she and Figaro worry about the danger to their happiness in terms of mockery presented by the Count. The music tells us about Figaro's shrewdness, his liveliness and his appetite for action; but by the end of the duet, Figaro finds himself singing Susanna's tune as he determines to foil his master, following her superior perceptions. The point, made in every performance, is in the music and needs no verbal explanation.

Similarly, critics have described *Don Giovanni* as the story of the fabulous libertine's failures; not one of the ladies wooed by him during the course of the work is actually seduced, and from this point of view he can be dismissed as a failure. But if we allow the music to make the true dramatic points, whenever he sings he triumphs. The result of 'La ci darem la mano' is that the peasant girl Zerlina yields her hand. When, mandoline in hand, he sings his serenade, we find him totally irresistible.

Like *Le Nozze di Figaro*, *Don Giovanni* is an opera of dramatic, symphonically constructed ensembles. Both Don Giovanni and his supernatural antagonist are stinted of arias—the Don himself has only one, 'Finch' han dal vino', which after all is not concerned with the central passion of his life but only with a secondary pleasure. For the rest, his primacy is established in the ensembles which make him dominant in evil, unconventional, wilfully defying morality and heroically bent on his own damnation. Critics who feel that he should justify in action his reputation for endless amorous successes forget that it is almost brutally established in Leporello's 'Catalogue aria', and pay too little attention to his evil courage and flamboyant gaiety, qualities manifested in his dealings with all the characters no matter what his relation to them. The statue of

Teresa Saporiti, who was the original Donna Anna in Don Giovanni.

112

the Commendatore is left to destroy him with no musical resources except an unshakeable foundation in the key of D minor, from which he does not stray far.

The nineteenth century exalted *Don Giovanni* above Mozart's other operas because good is seen to triumph over evil in circumstances which can be regarded as tragic, for Don Giovanni seems, as the work unfolds, to possess every gift except that of love. The twentieth century has found in it a tortuous psychology of the composer: Don Giovanni kills the father of Donna Anna, and Wolfgang Amadeus Mozart, by separating himself from his own father and his father's interests, committed an act comparable to murder. Mozart, the argument goes, in his conscious, planning mind—that of an almost exemplary son—seems to have felt no sense of guilt about his relationship with Leopold, merely an occasional sadness that Leopold was unreasonable about Constanze and

The ballroom scene from an 1867 production of Don Giovanni *at Her Majesty's Theatre, London.*

their way of life. The splendour of reasoning from Freudian premises is that the motives and expressions of an unconscious mind need no evidence but can be assumed simply for the sake of argument. Mozart's letters do not indicate that he was conscious of any guilt towards the father whose advice and way of life he rejected—not even that he resented his father's unwillingness to look after their children while Wolfgang and Constanze went to make their fortune in England. The relationship between Don Giovanni and his destroyer, the statue of the Commendatore, is created with marvellous and fearsome vividness, but although musically it punishes a dissolute, chromatic villain through a diatonic D minor avenger from a supernatural world, it is surely only Mozart the dramatist rising to the climax of a drama, not the son repenting a crime towards his own father. The dramatist's participation in his work is made more intense through its appeal to his imagination than is suggested by the notion that passages of extreme intensity must necessarily symbolise the inner drama of an unconscious guilt. Actually, the opera does not emphasise Don Giovanni's awareness of his victim as a father; to him, the interruption of an attempted seduction by an old man with a sword is simply a nuisance, and commentators have always found the attitude of Donna Anna, saved by her father's death, oddly extreme. They do less than justice to the fact that Mozart was a dramatist whose drama was never entirely dependent on words. The Commendatore has to die so that he can destroy the libertine, and though Mozart creates the agony of his death with great intensity the Commendatore has already established himself, in musical terms, as the power capable of destroying the heroic sinner.

It is perhaps doubtful whether seeing *Don Giovanni* through Freudian symbolism adds anything to the effect of the work. Its greatness depends on the ability of its composer to enter with complete sympathy into all the varieties of experience which da Ponte assimilated in his text. Don Ottavio is the least effective of operatic tenors, but though dramatically redundant he is musically as convincingly real as the deplorable Leporello. Zerlina, initially led astray by Don Giovanni's craft and his social standing, learns from experience that her almost boorish Masetto is as lovable as the aristocratic seducer. Mozart approaches the opera as a work about life rather than as a work in which his own guilt can be exorcised. He can create a convincing Don Giovanni, just as he could create a convincing Cherubino, because he was a highly sexed young man orthodox enough to accept the notion that the only thing a highly sexed young man can do is marry. The libretto itself is less than perfect: the actual course of events is not deployed as logically and as clearly as the more complex plot of *Le Nozze di Figaro*, and Mozart's additional work on it for the Vienna production of 1788 added to the problems; for example, Don Ottavio was given the aria 'Dalla sua pace' to replace the splendid but extremely difficult 'Il mio tesoro', but which of the two beautiful arias does a director choose to omit? The tenor will do all he can to be allowed to sing both, so that the actual mechanics of when and where incidents take place is further confused. The power and strength of the music enable the work to triumph over a confused time-scheme, but the opera is a source of agitation for directors; da Ponte, writing libretti for three composers at once, did not achieve with *Don Giovanni* the success that had marked *Le Nozze di Figaro* and was to mark *Così fan Tutte* in 1790.

Così fan Tutte is an entirely conventional farcical comedy, as geometrically designed as a theorem by Euclid and, consequently, concerned with comic effects rather than with human truth. Guglielmo and Ferrando are engaged to, and deeply in love with, the sisters Fiordiligi and Dorabella; the sisters are equally devoted to them. Don Alfonso, older and less romantic in outlook, sets a test of fidelity: the two young men will go off, apparently to war, immediately returning in disguise, each to attempt to win the other's fiancée. Ferrando encounters impassioned opposition from Fiordiligi; Guglielmo has less difficulty in winning Dorabella. After farcical mock-suicides, each of the heroes wins round his friend's fiancée. The plot is explained and the girls forgiven, because '*così fan tutte*'—'that is what they all do'. Mozart of course points out, but the stage personalities do not notice, that the men are as eager for each other's lovers as they are for their own.

This extremely artificial work is Mozart's most sumptuously beautiful opera. Its action takes place in Naples, and Mozart's music evokes landscape, sunshine and Mediterranean evening. The lovers seem incapable of expressing themselves with less than extreme sensual delight, and we come to recognise that da Ponte's conventional study in easy cynicism is turned by Mozart into

The final scene from Don Giovanni, *in which the statue of the Commendatore comes to supper.*

an important human statement about love, fidelity and the dangers of a romantic attitude to life. If the greatest and most rewarding thing the quartet of romantics can do is to love, it matters little who is to be loved. The men, in a sense victorious, are at the same time defeated and, like the characters in any true classic comedy, they are wiser and better for the experiences they have undergone. Mozart analyses the type of love they desire and experience, and does so with amused and compassionate understanding. If this is what they all do, they mean no harm by it, and the real cause of infidelity and fickleness is the foolishly romantic belief that love exists irrespective of personality. Mozart's music always reflects emotional ambiguity, an awareness of the sorrow of happiness and the happiness of sorrow; we are never quite sure of his own attitude to the play of sunshine and shadows in his scores, for he is, in the last analysis, writing about the mixed experience which is life. Because of this, he could transform the shallow farce of *Così fan Tutte*, in which the personalities are not essentially human beings but only puppets used to work out an artificial theorem, into a work of human truth. Mozart decided that love could be passionately sincere though it lacked thought or judgement (for the ultimate cynicism of the opera lies in the total sincerity of its quartet of lovers), but as such it was no more than self-indulgence—and the self-indulgence is displayed by the florid beauty of the ambivalent love music. This is not a Keatsian work in which all we need to know is the identity of truth and beauty, for beauty, in *Così fan Tutte*, is an irresistible drug which we take to blind us to reality. It is an opera about the follies of self-deception.

Così fan Tutte was produced in January 1790. A year later the comedian–theatre manager–playwright Emanuel Schikaneder, whom Mozart had first met in his Salzburg days, took control of the Theater auf der Wieden, a new theatre in a working-class suburb of Vienna. He offered Mozart the libretto of a new, not yet written opera, *Die Zauberflöte*. This was to be a magic opera, a fantastic, elaborate pantomime designed to appeal not only to the sophisticatedly musical but also to a naive, working-class audience, particularly through a richly comic role for Schikaneder himself. Mozart was at first reluctant to involve himself in a magic opera, a type of work of which he had no experience, but he was won over when he learned that within the comic framework was to be a deep, earnest parable for Freemasons. Schikaneder, like Mozart, was a Mason; the comedy was to convey the doctrine and the spirit of their order, and the postulant's initiation into its mysteries would provide the hidden drama of the work.

The development of the libretto presented a number of problems. For one thing, its purpose as a parable had to take second place to its function as an effective source of profit. How much of it was the work of Schikaneder, an experienced provider of easy fun, and how much of its serious undercurrent was provided by Carl Ludwig Giesecke, a young recruit to his company who eventually became a professor of minerology, is a question not likely now to be answered; other Masons, including, apparently, Mozart himself, had a hand in devising the entertainment.

From the point of view of design, the text is a muddle. Tamino, a young Japanese prince (whose nationality is a complete irrelevance) is rescued by three ladies from the attacks of a monstrous serpent; they are servants of the Queen of the Night. They show Tamino a portrait of the Queen's daughter, Pamina, with which he immediately falls in love, and tell him that the daughter has to be rescued from an evil magician, Sarastro. The Queen of the Night herself appears to reinforce their pleas. A simple, cowardly, deceitful child of nature, Papageno, who has claimed to have saved Tamino's life by killing the serpent, is enrolled with the Prince in the task of rescuing

The sisters Dorabella and Fiordiligi in a scene from the 1972 Sadler's Wells Opera revival of Così fan Tutte.

116

Above: Part of the original score of Die Zauberflöte: *Tamino's aria 'Dies Bildnis ist bezaubernd schön' (O loveliness beyond compare), sung when he is first shown the portrait of Pamina by the servants of the Queen of the Night.*

Left: Emanuel Schikaneder, the talented theatre manager, comedian, playwright and librettist of Die Zauberflöte, *who became a close friend of the Mozarts. (From an engraving by Löschenkohl.)*

Above right: Emanuel Schikaneder as Papageno, in the first production of Die Zauberflöte *in 1791.*

Pamina, and they set out on their adventure after Tamino has been given a magic flute and Papageno a magic glockenspiel to aid them. Tamino soon discovers that Sarastro represents enlightenment, humanitarian wisdom and goodness while it is the Queen who belongs to the realms of darkness, ignorance and obscurantism. Papageno, whose only desire is for a suitable wife, is led through elementary ordeals until, disappointed to the verge of suicide, he finds his love. Tamino and Pamina, who have now met and fallen in love, follow a sterner course of initiation into Sarastro's brotherhood; in the end, darkness is vanquished, and the two reach the glory of enlightenment.

The apparent change of direction which turns the story upside down and makes good and evil change places would probably not worry a listener who had read no commentaries but simply, like the audience at the Theater auf der Wieden, went to see a show. There are possible reasons, such as their lack of any individuality, for not believing in the Queen's attendants and their story. The Queen herself is not in the same order of being as other characters, but communicates with the world in thrilling but entirely artificial coloratura brilliancies, rising to stratospheric heights with the utmost vocal agility, far removed from simple humanity. Three genii, small boys whose services are normally at the command of Sarastro, are creatures of absolute innocence. Sarastro is patently good, communicating in music of great, solemn nobility; his, wrote Bernard Shaw, is the only music which could fittingly be sung by the voice of God. Whatever confusions exist in a libretto not entirely serious in intention—the manager–comedian was obviously determined to secure every possible laugh and fit all his favourite tricks into the action—were not in the mind of its composer, whose music created the spirit of the work and gives it complete musical coherence within the widest possible variety of style and incident. The magic flute itself represents good, but it is the gift of the Queen of the Night,

119

presented by her attendant ladies: if this is a contradiction, the presentation is made to the accompaniment of a musical phrase which becomes Sarastro's in his sublime hymn invoking the blessing of Isis and Osiris on Tamino and Pamina. It is music which gives *Die Zauberflöte* its coherence

Above: A play-bill for the first performance of Die Zauberflöte *at the Theater auf der Wieden in 1791.*
Right: The final scene from the 1974 Covent Garden production of La Clemenza di Tito, *and (inset) the same scene in a design by Fuentes for an early production at* La Scala, Milan.

The ground plan of No. 970, Rauhensteingasse, Vienna, where Mozart spent the last year of his life, and (below) the room in which he died.

and its meaning, just as it is the music of *Don Giovanni* which allows us to see the Don as the supreme seducer though we are not privileged to watch any of his seductions.

Mozart imposes coherence upon materials of the utmost diversity. Papageno's music has the easy simplicity of folk-song, the music of Sarastro's temple has a unique solemnity. The wicked negro, Monostatos, with his designs upon Pamina's virtue, is never allowed to become a mere caricature of evil, and Pamina, driven to desperation by the strife between Sarastro and her mother, faces the depths of Mozartian despair in an aria in G minor before Tamino leads her to glory through the perilous ordeal by fire and water. Their last guides are Two Men in Armour, who sing a Lutheran chorale treated in strict counterpoint like a chorale prelude by Bach (whose music, in 1782, was the last great revelation Mozart was to receive), and the two go through their final ordeal to music of the barest simplicity—a solemn march played by Tamino's flute accompanied only by sombre chords from the brass underlaid by ominous drum-beats. Earlier in the opera, when Tamino sits alone outside the temple of Sarastro, the world of Wagner suddenly draws near in its atmosphere and its treatment of a German text in accompanied recitative.

All ends in happiness: even Papageno receives as much enlightenment as his nature can receive after his final ordeal; his Papagena lost, he suffers as Pamina suffers in her G minor aria. Papageno is by nature funny, so that his comic despair is, perhaps, the most tragic music in the score because it is a clown's tragedy. But Mozart's intentions are left for us to interpret for ourselves; even commentators who have painstakingly studied the doctrines of Freemasonry in Mozart's time are not unanimous about the precise Masonic points the opera wishes to make: they concern, perhaps, the position of women in a totally male society—or perhaps the withdrawal of toleration for Freemasonry after the death of Joseph II. The Queen of the Night may be a memory of Maria Theresa, who hated Freemasonry. But all this, perhaps, is irrelevant. The opera is about initiation into humanitarian wisdom, and about the necessity of human love. The duet sung by Papageno and Pamina early in the action is about love not as a direct human experience but as a necessary ideal: man and wife together reach towards divinity; it is Tamino and Pamina together who reach enlightenment. It is Mozart's last statement on human love, which was the theme of all his operas. Musically, the work is Mozart's ultimate synthesis, dedicated to the idea of love as the way to the greatest good.

Die Zauberflöte was almost complete when, in July 1791, *La Clemenza di Tito* was commissioned to celebrate the coronation of Leopold II in Prague. Mozart was given less than two months in which to complete the work. The libretto was by Metastasio, set some twenty times before by earlier composers and rather casually revised in a way that offered Mozart no opportunities for dramatic, musically active, symphonic ensembles. It remained traditional old-fashioned *opera seria*, sacrificing Mozart's genius for characterisation in support of the old aesthetic which regarded the *dramatis personae* as representatives of fixed emotions. The recitatives were composed by Mozart's pupil Süssmayr (who was to complete the *Requiem* six months later), and Mozart wrote arias and choruses of splendid richness and intensity, again too detailed and powerful for untutored ears, for the new Empress described the work as 'German piggishness' after arriving late with the Emperor for the first performance. The world did not, however, agree with her. The circumstances of its ceremonial first night on 6 September 1791 were against it, but thereafter it was widely produced and enjoyed by audiences who had not lost their affection for its traditional style. *Die Zauberflöte* was produced on 30 September and rapidly became the greatest success of Mozart's life. Two months later, on 5 December, Mozart died.

9 Mozart's Musical World

To discuss Mozart's work genre by genre would be simply to repeat what has been written many times before. Mozart is the touchstone for those who write about music: commentators refer to his work to justify and explain whatever principles they uphold. Whatever quality we wish to exalt can be found in his work—its immaculate technique, its infallible sense of balance and proportion, its untiring vitality, its eloquence and its excitement—so that every age since 1791 has found Mozart the exponent of the qualities it most desires.

Mozart's symphonies, in the 1780s, had ceased to be based on single themes representing first and second subjects, just as in these later symphonies he anticipated the problems of composers who felt that sonata form, by giving the first movement a work's strongest intellectual and emotional framework, tended to lead to symphonic anti-climaxes. Mozart found that sonata form was elastic enough to allow all the movements of his later symphonies except the minuet to be written in first-movement form without any danger of monotony, applying the intellectual strength and innate drama of sonata form to an entire work while providing sufficient variety to give each work a vast breadth of outlook such as that of the 'Jupiter' Symphony. As the later symphonies depend on subject groups rather than subject phrases, so that each symphony is likely to present thematic paragraphs rather than thematic sentences, the last movement of the Jupiter provides four themes in C major, its tonic, and two in G major as the second group. None of these themes extends to a full-grown melody, but each is a phrase; all except the first have great energy and purposefulness, but the first is simply a phrase of four semibreves—C, D, F, E—which contrapuntal composers, Bach among them, had used before. They turned up, too, in Mozart's first and thirty-third symphonies, and in a Mass (K. 192) of 1774, where they are sung, in the Creed, to the word *credo* ('I believe'). It seems that the four-note phrase had some special significance for Mozart, for not only is it a statement of faith in the Mass, but in the 'Jupiter' Symphony it becomes a powerful stabilising force. The whole finale is a dazzling display of contrapuntal brilliance, and all the material of the two subject groups is used in fugal style. Each makes sense when it is inverted, which adds to the complexity of the material and of the work's vision. We are presented with a creative vision of complex, urgent and powerful musical entities all diverse but all related, a musical solar system balanced in orbit round the axis of the four semibreves.

Mozart's symphonies tend to begin with a musical call to attention which is immediately followed by a phrase—answer or theme—played quietly. First subjects are usually commanding and masculine, while important material in the second subject group is normally lyrical and 'feminine'. Traditional analysis of Mozart's work has rightly stressed the diversity and contrast of material involved in his symphonic expositions. But at the same time this powerfully contrasting material paradoxically forms a unity, though the unity may be hidden. A symphony by Haydn often sets out to show the possibilities of variety and contrast possible in a single theme, so that a second subject is clearly a variant of a first: the fundamental unity of Mozart's materials is never clearly shown, as though the composer wishes it to be sensed rather than analysed.

When Mozart signals an urgent musical crisis at the opening of the development section of the last movement of the G minor Symphony (K. 550), the crisis seems to undermine our basic sense of tonality. By using eleven of the twelve notes of the chromatic scale in a jagged, distorted rhythm as an extension of the movement's strongly tonal first subject, he is depriving us of any strong sense of a home key to which we can refer. It is as though he is anticipating the 'note row' technique of Schoenberg and twentieth-century composers.

Schoenberg's twelve-note method of composition replaced the traditional diatonic major or minor scale as the basis of a work by setting out all the twelve semitones as a series, created for an individual work and invariable for that work. In this way the composer makes music from possible permutations and combinations of the series and its permissible disguises: it can be inverted, so that the intervals are made to rise when, in its original form, they fall, and vice versa; it can be retrograde (played backwards); and its inversion can be played backwards. We learn to listen to this music not through concentration on the relationship within a key of the notes forming it, but through the intervals between the notes themselves.

The development section of the finale of the G minor Symphony uses the notes of the chromatic scale in a single destructive figure, distorting the first subject of the music as it does so. This is not the only passage by Mozart to use all the notes of the entire chromatic scale; it is the most challenging, however, and it is a statement of music in extreme peril. Out of this, having presented music analogous to a Schoenbergian series, and by serial methods of organisation and permutation, Mozart rebuilds the sense of tonality destroyed by the series.

But he often uses less all-inclusive phrases. The G minor Symphony begins with an urgent, pounding theme in the violins, a semitone descent, E flat to D, repeated three times and followed by a leap of a sixth, from D to B flat; it then descends by thirds—B flat to G, G to E flat, E flat to C; it is accompanied by throbbing violas, which are playing B flat and G a third below alternating with B flat and G a sixth above. Sixths and thirds, without rhythm or any other melodic life, are not enough to give a movement character, but their presence as a basic unit of organisation gives them the power to reinforce the nature of the music. The second subject, when it arrives, is outlined by a sixth—its first note is F and its penultimate A, while within the phrase, which climbs from B flat to G, is its essential melodic ingredient; incidentally, it includes a fall of a third. The inner unity is served by these ingredients, which do not sound like each other and which are totally different in rhythm and gait.

Similar coincidences—if they are not precise and conscious designs—are part of Mozart's thought, increasingly exploited as he became increasingly fascinated by polyphonic and contrapuntal styles within a symphonic framework. Other works of all sorts show similar underlying unifying factors, but the dramatic point of contrast and resolution exists in Mozart's work in a unity which is often not so much hidden as subliminal. He was, however, so complete and conscious an artist that it is unwise to speculate about instinctive elements in his work.

If we realise that Mozart's music is most expressive when it is at its most intellectual (the processes of thought in his music represent not a withdrawal of emotion but an intensification of emotion which inspires keener thought), we can understand the special glory of such movements as the great operatic ensembles, the finales of the G minor and 'Jupiter' Symphonies. The technical magnificence of such music is the means by which it achieves its power, and that power is not a means of subduing us or leading us to consider our own insignificance in the face of its majesty; it is a power in which we are invited to participate—it belongs to the humanity we share. The philosopher Bernard Williams, speaking in a broadcast about the A major Symphony (K. 201),

Original manuscript of the Lacrymosa from Mozart's
Requiem, *on which he was working when he died.*

said: 'If one had no limitations, no stupidities, no anxieties, this is what thinking would be like.' Mozartian thinking—and no composer was a deeper, more clear-sighted thinker—is a process of beautiful exactitude, elegant precision and great clarity; it is always exhilarating because it reaches incontrovertible solutions, and it always involves emotional power. The unemotional 'cold' thinker is, we learn from Mozart, less than a complete man. Whenever Mozart involves himself in a particularly demanding musical form (the choral preludes of the Masonic Funeral Music, K. 477, the music of the Two Armed Men in *Die Zauberflöte*, and the Lacrymosa of the *Requiem*, for instance) he does so not simply because such forms are powerful and impressive in themselves, but because only powerful, impressive forms can embody the statements he has to make.

Not that Mozart ceased to think elegantly and exactly when working in a more relaxed style. Of all the forms he handled, only one, the piano concerto, can in any sense be said to be his invention: his handling of this is unique. An early piano concerto, K. 39, is simply an arrangement of music by J. C. Bach in which he gave orchestral accompaniment to music for clavier. The form, since the passing of the concerto grosso period, was poised uneasily between the concerto principles of the baroque composers and a new, symphonic-style concerto. The baroque concerto had established its key and its principle material, a ritornello, which recurred to hold the movement together. The rise of the sonata principle made it possible for composers to regard the soloist's own thematic contribution as a second subject; while its first subject could function in a manner comparable to the traditional ritornello, the development section could work on the 'ritornello' and on the soloist's theme, and a recapitulation could then bring the movement to a sonata-style conclusion.

The problems arising from the hybrid concerto form, as Mozart became aware of them, concerned the position of the soloist as hero of the work and focus of the audience's attention. Mozart was an unashamedly dazzling virtuoso who knew, for a start, that he could demonstrate his pre-eminence by the brilliance of his playing, and do so without reducing the power of the orchestra. He discovered that to concentrate too exclusively on the soloist—allowing him, for example, to demand the first word and usurp the ritornello's traditional function—was ultimately to reduce his authority by removing the real confrontation of orchestra and soloist. There is no achievement in dominating those who stand in the shadow.

In Mozart's hands the concerto was always an equal partnership of soloist and orchestra, in which the soloist's powers of display and fertility of imagination are balanced by an orchestra which provides the original, and essentially important, topic for discussion and thus stimulates or provokes the soloist's inventive powers. Only in the E flat Concerto (K. 271) is the pianist introduced at the beginning of the work, to answer the orchestra's announcement of the work's key. The exposition of the first-subject ritornello music follows after the piano has imposed its presence on the structure, and thus, though the Concerto is the first mature work Mozart achieved in the form, the orchestra is essentially diminished. Mozart's answer to the problem of the soloist's status was to emphasise his creative role, to show him responding to the ritornello with a flood of exciting ideas. In the mature concertos which Mozart wrote in Vienna, most as centre-pieces for his own concerts, it is misleading to write of their first movements in symphonic terms of first or second subjects, of ritornello or of solo theme. The plan analysed as ritornello–exposition–ritornello – development – recapitulation – ritornello, which applies quite adequately to the concertos of Beethoven, oversimplifies the Mozart concertos because Mozart's fertility of invention deploys quite extensive groups of contrasted themes, used in a variety of ways as the composer applies them to the exposition–development–recapitulation pattern. There are six important themes exposed in the E flat Concerto, and all six are laid out in the introduction: the first and second of them are defined as important in the soloist's exposition; the orchestra's first ritornello deals mainly with the fifth, the development with the second and third; the sixth theme is presented in the introduction and then reserved for the conclusion of the movement, to be a final clinching point. In any concerto, Mozart decided, there would be themes not shared by piano and orchestra, but which these were would be worked out as the movement progressed; the outcome was not a matter of convention but of the apparently spontaneous evolution of these materials according to the inner law of their own being.

The concertos for other instruments, even so miraculous a work as the Clarinet Concerto (K. 622), maintain the hybrid semi-symphonic form, but the piano concertos which follow K. 271 have music of great thematic richness and freedom based on the interaction and development of six or more themes, one or more of which might be reserved for the orchestra while one or more might belong exclusively to the piano—obeying what seem to be laws deduced from their own individual nature and their relation to each other. The other movements of the Mozart piano concertos are given equal freedom; slow movements turn the solo instrument into a singer of great lyrical and expressive range; the music becomes analogous to a concert aria in its extent and variety. At other times, in the movements which Mozart called 'Romanze', they achieve a perfect song-like simplicity in which the soloist leads and controls orchestral richness without forfeiting natural ease of utterance. The finale is usually a rondo, and in Mozart's hands the rondo, its essential theme twice yielding to episodes in contrasted keys, refuses as firmly as his first movement to be subdued to any formula. Given the ritornello or refrain-like nature of the main theme, the amount of weight allowed to rest—or forced upon—the episodes depends always upon their individual character and their context in the movement. More than any of his other works, the piano concertos seem to create themselves from their own material; they accept formal discipline, but its demands are never dictatorial.

If the major forms—symphony, concerto, string quartet, string quintet and opera—show Mozart's music combining the most intense power of organisation with the greatest degree of communication, these forms do not exhaust the fascination or the greatness of his music. Mozart was deliberately, as much by nature as by profession, an entertainer, who never regarded the entertainment of his audience as a trivial side of his work to be treated casually. A work like the Oboe Quartet (K. 370) is essentially a lighter work than any of the string quartets dedicated to Haydn because the great intensities of thought are not stimulated into action; the oboe's individual colour alone makes it a soloist. When Mozart added a wind instrument to strings in a chamber work, he seemed to find the qualities of sound and colour created by such ensembles inspiration enough to motivate the music he was writing. Only the marvellous Clarinet Quintet (K. 581) reaches towards typical Mozartian intensities, for Mozart never shared the modern belief that music should always aim at supreme heights of emotion; it was the means of expression for all his moods, whatever their circumstances. When Constanze could not find the ribbon she intended to wear for an outing and kept her husband waiting while she searched for it, it was quite natural for him to use this as the occasion of a setting for soprano, tenor, bass and strings, 'Liebes Mandel, wo ist Bandel', K. 441 ('Dear girl, where's your ribbon?'). The ordeal by fire and water in *Die Zauberflöte* is amongst the world's greatest music, but composing it was no more effort to him than composing the comic quartet, 'Caro mio, Druck und Schluck', K. App. 5, or contriving part songs on scandalous texts. Mozart, as we have seen, delighted in puns

The opening of the Paris Symphony, K. 297, in Mozart's manuscript score.

and nonsense rhymes, and invented ridiculous nicknames for his friends; he never reserved music, his natural means of expression, for moods of special dignity or seriousness. Music and life, at whatever level they met, were inseparable in his mind.

The title 'symphony' was clearly associated in Haydn's mind with a close and intellectual working out of materials not always serious or solemn—many are plainly comic—but always posing musical questions of some moment; titles like serenade, divertimento and *Feldpartita* imply that Haydn intends to relax and entertain. Mozart's music does not fit into easy categories. The word 'serenade' implies for him not the mood of a work but the number of movements it occupies or the type of orchestration it requires.

Of the serenades only *Eine kleine Nachtmusik*, Mozart at his most exquisitely natural, is widely known, but the idea of the serenade, with style and instrumentation often more freely organised than in other forms, seems often to have stimulated the composer to moods of simple beauty—happiness shot like silk with regret or sorrow. But among the serenades, to make generalisation impossible, is the amazing work in C minor, K. 388, composed in 1782 for two oboes, two clarinets, two bassoons and two horns. This is one of the most tense, dramatic and poignant of all Mozartian expressions of distress. It is a work to which we cannot attribute any occasion or special purpose, and its scoring has a rare bite and toughness. Mozart himself rearranged the work as a string quintet, K. 406, but like most of Mozart's revisions of his own works these second thoughts lack the tension and toughness of the original instrumentations. The work is the antithesis of anything we usually understand by the word 'serenade'.

It is significant of Mozart's personality and attitude to music that we never suspect him of any lack of sympathy in music he wrote simply for money. As a solo instrument the flute did not please him, but it would be hard to detect this from any work in which he uses the flute as soloist.

It never stimulates him to any of the miraculous, or near miraculous, feats that he achieved with piano, clarinet or strings. But the Concerto for flute and harp (K. 299) offers nothing but delight, charm and skilled craftsmanship; it was part of Mozart's professional duty to know the things that a flute—or any instrument whether he cared for it or not—could do with grace and charm. Mozart wrote more 'great' music than almost any other composer, but this music is not necessarily charming—one is moved and disturbed, one's spirit is enlarged, by greatness; charm, to Mozart, is a secondary though admirable quality.

In one sense, little of Mozart's work was written entirely for his own satisfaction. As a professional writer he had always to take into account the tastes and idiosyncracies of patrons, performers and librettists. In the early string quartets, thirteen works written before 1773, he was exploring a popular form which it was necessary for him to master because it commanded a very large body of amateur performers. But it is the six String Quartets dedicated to Haydn, composed between 1782 and 1785, which exist in complete freedom from any outside pressures, precisely as Mozart wished them to exist: they range from 'The Hunt', K. 458, a work of lively, natural grace and charm (it is the fourth of the six) to the C major Quartet, K. 465 (the last), known as the 'Dissonance' Quartet for its disturbing harmonic unease in a strangely puzzling introduction. Such works represent the mind of a composer taking no heed of particular players or patrons but facing the demands of personal expression in complete freedom. Mozart's last three string quartets, K. 575, K. 589 and K. 590, were commissioned in 1789 by the King of Prussia, an enthusiastic and (judging by the music Mozart wrote for him) accomplished cellist; no practical composer—and musically, it cannot be said too often, Mozart was always practical—would write string quartets for a cello-playing monarch without taking care that His Majesty had music of authority and interest to play, even though this meant that the composer must rethink some of the traditional notions of quartet writing.

The genesis of the four string quintets which Mozart wrote between 1787 and his death is more mysterious. An early quintet K. 174, composed in 1773, is typical of Mozart's eagerness to try everything, and the string version of the great C minor Wind Serenade (K. 388) suggests, according to Einstein, that the death of Frederick the Great and the accession of his cello-playing son prompted Mozart to think of music in which a cello could take part. The new king appointed Luigi Boccherini, composer of beautifully written string quintets less personal and emotionally charged than Mozart's, to be Prussian court composer, and it may be (as Einstein believed) that this inspired Mozart to begin work on a set of six string quintets (the conventional number for a group of works) to dedicate to the King, who apparently enjoyed quintets, but never finished them.

Mozart always liked to have music as a guide to what might be done with any form, but had nothing in this instance to give him any precise lead. He chose, perhaps because of his affection for the viola, perhaps to give a potential royal patron a more outstanding role, to add a viola part to the basic quartet, as Boccherini did; apart from that, these quintets are entirely personal, portraying the special Mozartian features of emotional ambiguity in which each experience seems to involve its contrary emotion, as though joy and sorrow exist interdependently, the one impossible without the other. Of the five he completed, the G minor Quintet (K. 516) belongs to the world of desperation and tragedy to be explored further in the G minor Symphony (K. 550) some time later, but with a sense of submission to tragedy which the Symphony refuses to make. The previous quintet, in C major (K. 515), has a slow movement in which the two violas are used to create a marvellously rich texture, seeming always to add questions, hesitations, uncertainties and modifications to the apparently spontaneous intensities of the first violin.

But the fact that Mozart was a professional composer, writing for the most part the music for which patrons asked and paid rather than the music which he might have chosen to write were he free from economic pressures, never hides the personality of his music. The idea of self-expression applied to Mozart means that whatever task came his way stimulated music, because music was his language; therefore any task could arouse his deepest, most intense feelings. The large number of church works which he wrote before 1781 was the result of a stream of commissions which dried up when he left Salzburg; in Vienna, Joseph II forbade the use of the orchestra in church so that there was no occasion for new settings of the Mass and the liturgy in general during the rest of Mozart's life. To some extent, music for Masonic Lodges and their ceremonies replaced church music in Mozart's output after he was granted membership of the Viennese Lodge 'Zur Wohltätigkeit' (Benevolence) in December 1784.

Maria Theresa's banning of Freemasonry, which she had detested, was relaxed by Joseph II, and a large number of aristocrats and intellectuals openly became members of Austrian lodges, among them Wolfgang and Leopold Mozart and the devoutly Catholic Haydn, though neither of the two elder composers seemed to regard Freemasonry as more than a social organisation; to Wolfgang, however, it was a powerful stimulus. Just as human suffering suggested to him the key of G minor, and tragic passion belonged to D minor, the numinous solemnities of Masonry suggested music in E flat, a choice of key which adds

Overleaf: Two pages from Mozart's own catalogue of his compositions. (Left) Dating from February to April 1784, this shows the Piano Concertos in E flat, in B flat and in D major, K. 449–51; the Quintet for piano and wind instruments, K. 452; and the Piano Concerto in G major, K. 453. (Right) The opening of the Masonic Cantata, K. 619, is followed by early work on Die Zauberflöte—the *Overture, the March of the Priests and Tamino's entry in Act I.*

a mysterious element to the jubilant Symphony in E flat (K. 543). The solemn brass E flat chords which open *Die Zauberflöte* apparently belong directly to the ceremonial of a lodge meeting.

Only a few of Mozart's works refer explicitly to Masonic doctrine and practice, but no deep study of its inner significance is necessary to realise that his membership of the order gave him a profound intellectual and spiritual stimulus. To what extent Masonic doctrine took the place of the religion in which he had been brought up we cannot say, but there is evidence that he thought less of Catholicism in the closing years of his life than he had done as a youth, when he took it largely for granted. But in many ways the Catholic Church and Freemasonry are complementary in his music. A work like the *Maurerische Trauermusik* (Masonic Funeral Music), K. 477, could be played quite appropriately at a totally Christian mourning. Its dark-toned orchestra—no flutes, but heavy basset horns and double bassoon—shares the sombreness of the *Requiem*. Its form is that of a choral prelude with a brief prologue and epilogue; the theme elaborated is that of a Gregorian psalm chant, which naturally associates the music with the Catholic idea of death—which after all, may be representative of any other. The work commemorates two fellow-Masons of great social eminence—the Duke Georg August zu Mecklenburg Strelitz and Franz Count Esterhazy von Galantha. The music is profound, deeply felt, concentrated and powerful, and although it contains explicit reference to Masonic teaching, it remains a meditation of death in terms which musically are Christian and Catholic. In a letter to his father when Leopold was approaching death, Mozart, as a Mason, called death 'the doorway to true joy'; not a few Catholics might use the same description.

Many commentators have decided that the power and sublimity of Mozart's Masonic works exceeds that of his more conventional Christian music, and that his Catholicism was finally overruled by his adherence to Freemasonry. But the nature of music as Mozart created it seems to be far more self-sufficient. The qualities which drew him to his second religion apparently included its ritual presentation of rational eighteenth-century attitudes in terms paradoxically mystical, and its genuine rejection of the social hierarchies which Mozart refused to accept; in his own Lodge, or visiting other Lodges as a great musician, he was the equal of every other member. Freemasonry acted out the doctrines of equality promulgated in *Le Nozze di Figaro*: it was, in a sense, the religion of the Enlightenment, which motivated so much of Mozart's thought. As an individual considering human destiny, the composer might have found the end of Don Giovanni—the libertine dragged off to hell by Demons at the orders of a good Christian—to be comically superstitious, but as a highly imaginative musician he could take it quite seriously and prove it to be very frightening. Just as the inspiration of much of Mozart's greatest work seems to have been music itself and the desire to embody, organise and formulate musical ideas whatever their source, when his music reflects external ideas—Freemasonry, Catholic devotion and Christian humanitarianism among them—the ideas seem not to be developed in spite of or as an accompaniment to music, but to have grown out of the music itself. As in the materials of music, so in the realm of ideas, Mozart is the supreme synthesiser. As a great composer, he created a world of order and coherence. But that world is not simply the world of musical law: Mozart's musical law reflects the universal natural law—timeless, immutable, and true for whatever ideas he was called upon to handle.

10 The Legend

There is something fitting, as we have seen, in Mozart's story. In less than thirty-six years he had burned himself out and died, for whatever reason, a failure in any worldly sense. Obviously, his downfall needed explanation, and from the many attempts to find its cause comes the collection of Mozart myths which are still accepted today. Whatever cannot be explained in scientific or historical terms has to be explained through the creation of a myth, and throughout his life stories about Mozart abounded for the myth-makers: from his already quoted complaint at the age of eight that Madame de Pompadour refused to kiss him although the Empress had done so, to the scene in the last months of his life when, composing *Die Zauberflöte* in the garden house lent to him by Schikaneder, he and his wife were found dancing like children to keep themselves warm on a cold morning.

Nannerl wrote her reminiscences of her brother in the spring of 1792, concentrating on his life before he left Salzburg. She affected to know nothing of value about his marriage or his activities in Vienna, and her work was expanded by an anonymous writer equally hostile to Wolfgang's widow. 'Apart from his music', he writes, 'Mozart was almost always a child, and thus he remained.' Friedrich Schlichtegroll, who based the account of Mozart in his *Nekrolog* for 1791 on Nannerl's memories, apparently made some enquiries of his own and ended with praise of the unfortunate Constanze Mozart. 'She sought to restrain him from many foolishnesses and excesses. Despite a considerable income, and yet in consequence of his exceptional sensuality and domestic disorder, he left his family nothing beyond the glory of his name.' There is nothing in other writings to suggest that Schlichtegroll had any real evidence of Mozart's 'exceptional sensuality' in any sense that we could understand the term, but Constanze, in 1794, bought up an entire edition of the *Nekrolog* and obliterated this passage. Obviously,

Title-page of the Nekrolog *for 1791.*

though, if a celebrated composer with a 'considerable income' dies in abject poverty weighed down
by debts, the first guess anyone makes is Schlichtegroll's: perhaps it is more likely than the idea that
Mozart was a childlike innocent who could not
organise his life in any satisfactory way.

There is no evidence for any really concerted
attack on Mozart, most of whose contemporaries
saw him as quite humanly fallible. Michael Kelly
noted that the composer had a considerable appetite for punch, and Franz Seraph von Destouches,
who had known both Haydn and Mozart and
became Prince Wallerstein's *Kapellmeister*, noted
not only Mozart's passion for billiards (which he
played very badly) but also the high stakes he was
accustomed to play for. Destouches's reminiscences of Mozart appear in the diary of one Sul-
piz Boisserée of Stuttgart, and are so inaccurate
that it is hard to take anything he says seriously.
But the evaporation of Mozart's considerable
earnings could be explained by frenzied, compulsive gambling. This explanation was developed as
far as it could go by a German musicologist, Uwe
Kraemer, in the periodical *Musica* for May and
June 1976. The evidence, however, goes no further
than Destouches's single, untrustworthy statement, and Destouches does not explain why the
most unselfish of Mozart's friends, Puchberg, continually lent considerable sums to a man whom
he knew to have been only a permanently unlucky
but also a hopelessly compulsive gambler.

The myth of the childlike innocent reappeared
in Paris in 1804, when Jean-Baptiste-Antoine
Suard published his 'Anecdotes sur Mozart' in
volume five of his *Mélanges de Littérature*. Suard
declared that Mozart loved money but was always
generous and would both give without discrimi-
nation and spend without reason. He earned a
great deal of money but lived so improvidently

*The garden house in the suburb of Wieden, Vienna, which
was lent by Emanuel Schikaneder to Mozart and in which
he composed some of the music for* Die Zauberflöte. *Here
Wolfgang and Constanze were found dancing about like
children to keep themselves warm.*

that he left his wife with nothing but the manuscripts of his compositions. Deeply as Mozart loved his wife, Suard explained, he could not live without other attractive women and composed *Die Zauberflöte* because that was the price set by a prima donna on her person: poetic justice struck him down, and he died of the incurable disease with which she had infected him. This at least offers a reason for his early death no more unlikely than the alternative belief that he was poisoned by Salieri, Leopold II's *Kapellmeister*. But Suard himself admitted that the *Zauberflöte* story was very unlikely.

The legends which multiplied round his life quickly changed their tone to concentrate upon the sufferings of the childlike innocent persecuted by his resentful inferiors. The Bohemian writer Franz Xaver Niemetschek, in 1798, explained how Joseph II's Italian musicians tried to sabotage *Le Nozze di Figaro* until Mozart saved the work by appealing directly to the Emperor. The Irish tenor, Michael Kelly, however, mentioned the enthusiasm of orchestra and singers for the work when it was rehearsed. Niemetschek noted that Mozart often earned a great deal of money, but this reached him irregularly; the irregularity of his income and his wife's frequent pregnancies, together with the high cost of living in Vienna, made his financial downfall inevitable. At the same time, the salary of 800 gulden a year which he received as chamber composer to the Emperor from 1787 onwards was more than twice that of his father as vice-*Kapellmeister* at Salzburg; Leopold Mozart earned 300 florins a year, with a subsistence allowance of 54 florins. Mozart's salary from the Emperor, together with his freelance earnings, should have enabled him to live modestly but fruitfully. Any musician was expected to live modestly even if he worked among the splendours of the imperial court.

The fact that Mozart lived unwisely and improvidently was soon forgotten, as were the strange rumours of his disorderly, even disreputable life. Constanze herself, and others of Mozart's friends, suppressed them assiduously. By 1794, a calendar printed in Chemnitz noted that music by Mozart was all that people seemed to want to hear, and that concert and opera producers, like publishers, busily supplied the demand. The Chemnitz editor was unhappy about this, for he found Mozart's symphonies to be less marked by unity of style, clarity and directness than those of Haydn. But Constanze, who owned the great majority of Mozart's manuscripts and exploited them shrewdly, continued her policy of restoring Mozart's good name even to the point of expurgating his letters to her whenever expurgation seemed to be politic. The darker, more questionable sides of Mozart's character were piously suppressed, so that by the time Otto Jahn published his four-volume biography of the composer (it appeared between 1856 and 1859) Mozart was being depicted as an angelic victim of human insensitivity and callousness.

In the nineteenth century, this characterisation appeared to accord with the music. The nineteenth century could not see beyond the vast bulk of Beethoven's work, aggressive, powerful music which outgrew the Mozartian orchestra, expanded the musical time-scale—Beethoven's Third Symphony, composed only a dozen years after Mozart's death, is longer than almost any two symphonies by Mozart—and enlarged the orchestra because it was designed to be heard in auditoria built to the modern scale. Thus the orchestra of Mozart began to sound limpid, innocent and unsensational to ears full of the clamour of a Beethoven finale, with three trombones, piccolo, cymbals and bass drum. It was the 'simplicity' of this aspect of Mozart's music which, to the romantics, hid its intellectual strength and emotional intensity. Played in the wrong sort of auditorium, it offered listeners obsessed by Beethoven's music of tragic violence and triumph only symmetry and charm, formal precision and elegance. This was the aspect of Mozart's work which the nineteenth century loved, and it led to a neglect of other important aspects of his music.

Hector Berlioz, a fervent admirer of Mozart's operas.

by characters of great warmth, passion and humanity, but although as a conductor he was more concerned with Beethoven's symphonies than with anything written by Mozart, the later symphonies appeared in his concert programmes.

Eduard Hanslick, the critic now remembered for little more than his opposition to Wagner, obviously shared the general nineteenth-century misconception of Mozart's music. In a long review of Wagner's *Parsifal* in 1883, Hanslick declared that Wagner's technique of composition was too elaborately intellectual to appeal to listeners for long, and that *Parsifal* itself cried out for a simpler style: only a naive composer like Mozart could have done justice to the legend.

The nineteenth-century misconception of Mozart and his music means, of course, little more than that it is very difficult for anyone to see the work of the past except through the spectacles of his own period, even when those spectacles dis-

Richard Wagner, who promoted German interest in Mozart.

The list of subscribers to his concerts at the Tratt-nerhof in Vienna in 1784 contains a hundred and seventy-six names, and Mozart regarded that as a capacity audience. In such an auditorium Mozart's orchestration must have sounded almost uncomfortably powerful and forceful.

It is in the context of performances with, say, double woodwind and a modern complement of strings in a hall holding more than a thousand list-eners that the nineteenth century looked back to the Mozart symphonies as models of innocent simplicity, apparently not noticing the desperate force and energy which drives through the G minor Symphony (K. 550); Schumann described it as a work of 'Grecian lightness and grace'. Berlioz recognised Mozart as a great opera composer, but to him Mozart's operas were clubs with which to attack the insolent charlatans who garbled a master's music. By the time he was twenty-one, in 1834, Wagner made it his task to tell the German public that Mozart was a fine dramatic composer whose dramatic works were peopled

tort. In the nineteenth century the composer was no longer an indispensable functionary; he had no fixed social position, and he lived outside society, struggling without any assurance of success to find the audience and the following which would give his work its social justification. The nine-

The orchestra at the Dresden Opera House under Adolf Hasse (1699–1783) shows how the opera orchestra was transformed by Mozart in the last years of his life.

teenth-century artist could console himself for his own difficulties by remembering the apparently unmerited sufferings of Mozart. Finally, the romantic age was baffled by Mozart because his music never seemed to be a direct reflection of its composer's experience. Romantic artists (not only composers) and their critics expected any work of art to be closely associated with their lives, as Berlioz's *Symphonie Fantastique* grew from the

Diſtribution of the Orcheſtra at the Opera-Houſe

Directed by le Sr. Haſſe.

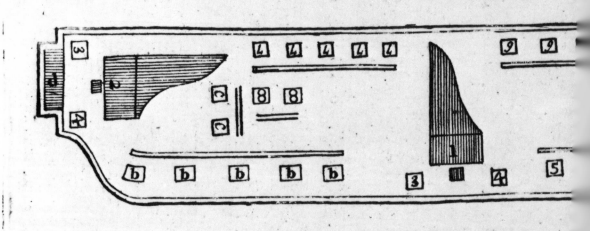

Explanation of the Cyphers.

1. Harpſichord of the Maſter de Chapelle.
2. Ditto of Accompaniment.
3. Violoncellos.
4. Counterbaſſes.
5. Firſt Violins.
6. Second Violins, with the Back towards the Theatre.

7. Hautbo
8. Flutes,
a. Tenors
b. Baſſoon
c. Huntin
d. A Tri
    anc

troubled love-life of the composer, or as Mahler's symphonies, so he claimed, were the continuing record of his spiritual experience. It was natural to his contemporaries that Wagner's love affair with Mathilde Wesendonck should be reflected in the passion and frustration of *Tristan und Isolde* and that the passion and frustration of the opera should motivate a similar love in its creator.

But Mozart, whose devotion to his wife was obviously deep and intense, simply wrote the greater part of a Mass in C minor (K. 417) in order to celebrate his love of and marriage to Constanze; we cannot particularly link the Mass to his marriage; more surprisingly we cannot link his marriage to the love songs of *Die Entführung aus dem Serail*, in which the hero Belmonte sings with splendid ardour of his love for another, fictitious Constanze. The songs are Belmonte's, not Mozart's, and attempts to find Mozart in his operas are as absurd as efforts to find the voice of Shakespeare in the soliloquies of Hamlet, Macbeth, King Lear or Othello.

In June 1783, while his wife in the next room was in labour with their first child, Raimund Leopold, Mozart wrote the first movement of the String Quartet in D minor (K. 421), and it would be hard to find any connection between that sinister music and the obviously important experience of becoming a father. In 1788, in a matter of some six weeks, Mozart completed his last three symphonies, each a world in itself. The E flat Symphony (K. 543) combines grace with strength, and rises above doubts and uncertainty into dazzling gaiety; it was completed on 26 June. The desperate, inconsolable G minor (K. 550), which submits its composer's music world to an enormous destructive strain, was completed on 25 July, and the mighty C major Symphony (K. 551) was finished on 10 August. If their composition was part of his plan for a series of subscription concerts which failed through lack of support, who, listening to them, would think so? But certainly while they were being composed Mozart wrote pathetic begging letters to his friend and fellow-Freemason Michael Puchberg. The destructive violence of the G minor seems to be about a vision of life more tragic than pathetic, and the E flat Symphony, like the Jupiter, reaches sublimities in which a serene power looks squarely at the possible darkness of life and dispels it.

In the closing months of 1789, when Mozart himself sometimes saw his situation as hopeless, he was occupied with what may be the most perfect

Drefden.

fame.

me.

me.

s.

n each Side for the Timballs

pets.

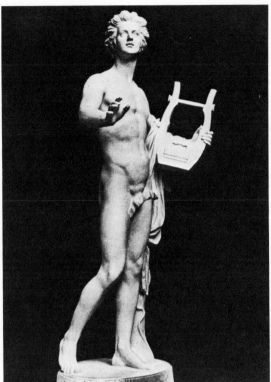

of his operas, *Così fan Tutte*, a cynical and mocking work which glitters with delight at the folly of trusting to human emotions. Mozart's personal despair does not intrude for a moment into the miraculous score of *Die Zauberflöte*, which sees life and morality as totally untouched by the personal miseries of poverty, desperation and failing health. He triumphantly justifies human life as it is lived by moral heroes who can face and overcome the forces of darkness. Mozart's music is music, not disguised autobiography. To find the creative personality behind it, just as to find Shakespeare's creative personality, one has to know Mozart's work and through this find the personality which created the huge, consistent picture of the entire human world and, whatever his circumstances, rejoiced in his power to do so.

Although Mozart's transcendence over personal experience was anything but easy for the nineteenth century to understand, its most percipient musicians adored Mozart's music for those elements of style which seemed to support the belief in Mozartian innocence and simplicity. *Così fan Tutte* fell from favour because, although its ironies are funny, they are unsparing and totally unromantic; the opera exposes the romantic view of life to ridicule. The two court operas, *Idomeneo* and *La Clemenza di Tito*, vanished from the stage. They were traditional *opera seria* and, in the eyes of the nineteenth century, dead because of the traditional techniques that were imposed upon them. The doctrine of Mozart's invincible innocence decided that the composer was not able to write cynically and that the flaw in the work was a libretto which did not really give Mozart the material he needed. Various efforts were made to fit the music to another, and innocuous, tale, but these too failed. Only *Die Entführung, Le Nozze di Figaro, Don Giovanni* and *Die Zauberflöte* remained as repertory pieces which deserved no special preparation, ready to be thrown on to the stage at almost any time. In Germany the two Italian works were given not only in German translation but with their recitatives turned into spoken dialogue. In the twentieth century *Idomeneo* came into its own. In England it was not produced until 1951, when audiences discovered that the conventions of *opera seria*, as Mozart handled them, were vigorously alive, so that the work has won audiences as large and devoted as any of Mozart's other operas. In 1973 *La Clemenza di Tito* was still regarded as an example of an outmoded style which not even Mozart could bring to life: in 1974, revived on the stage, the supposedly moribund opera became another masterly stage work— tense, expressive and dramatic, within a convention which the twentieth century finds it easy to accept.

In the same way, orchestras in the nineteenth century had tended to treat a few of the later and greater of Mozart's symphonies as easy light music while neglecting the rest; because these works are usually simpler in their demands on the harmonic memory, as we may call it, than those of Beethoven, and because their orchestration calls for fewer instruments, they were regarded as works through which any skilled orchestra could

A cartoonist's reaction to Gustav Mahler's intensely dramatic production of Don Giovanni *in Vienna, 1904.*

rattle with little demand for careful rehearsal, although in reality no music demands more exacting study or asks more precision. It is possible for the weight of a later orchestra to hide clumsy, awkward or unrehearsed playing; so much happens so loudly that some sense of excitement can be achieved in spite of a considerable degree of inaccuracy and less than ideal ensemble. But Bernard Shaw, writing in 1888 as 'Corno di Bassetto', the music critic of *The Star*, declared: 'Mozart can utterly baffle a band for which Beethoven, Berlioz and Wagner have no terrors. It is useless to try to make the G minor Symphony "go" by driving a too heavy body of strings through it with all the splendour and impetuosity of an Edinburgh express.' This, Shaw pointed out, was merely to repeat Wagner's complaint that 'many conductors always contrived to make Mozart's music sound vapid'. Their incapacity to grasp Mozart's strength and energy made them present the music as easy-going triviality.

The same frame of mind persuaded them that Mozart's instrumental music could be dismissed for any but teaching purposes. The musical child was not expected to face the challenges to his physical strength and his musical understanding presented by the piano music of Beethoven: Mozart's lighter style, with its transparencies of sound and its demands for grace, ease and the utmost sensitivity of phrasing, was held to be good for the technique of the child player but never to strain his musical understanding. The fact is that in many respects Beethoven's mind is not subtle, while Mozart's work presents unusual subtleties, demands exquisite phrasing and balance—the very qualities in fact which so often escape all but the most consummate musicians.

It is the twentieth century that has found in the music of Mozart an unparalleled range of the most intense emotional expression, from cheerful playfulness to wild hilarity, from great intellectual triumph to poignancies of love, from godlike, solemn serenity to desperate anguish, voicing all its emotions in forms which are manifestations of musical meanings.

As we have seen, legends are formed around the greatest men so that we may first understand them by recreating them in our own image. There is a new Mozart called into being by the musicologist H. C. Robbins Landon, who has found that Mozart was a socially progressive rebel, writing an opera about servants who defeat the machinations of masters far more powerful than they but morally and intellectually their inferiors, who found religious truth in the suspect doctrines of Freemasonry, who created the evil hero who obeys no power outside his own will, who mocked the idea of fidelity in love, and who is left to perish in neglect because the existence of his music is itself a rebellion against accepted standards. There is another Mozart, discovered by Brigid Brophy, whose work is a manifestation of Freudian complexities. Legends take the truth and exaggerate it to the point at which it is distorted. Our duty to Mozart, and to Music, and to ourselves, is to remove the myths, to find hidden behind them a singularly lovable man with at least his fair share of human failings—careless, improvident, extravagant, intolerant of inferior workmanship, but generous and affectionate. In many respects, perhaps, the most gifted man of whom we have any trustworthy detailed record.

145

Mozart's Life in Brief

1719 Birth of Leopold Mozart

1720 Birth of Anna Maria Pertl

1743 Appointment of Leopold Mozart as fourth violinist at the court of the Prince Archbishop of Salzburg

1747 Marriage of Leopold Mozart and Maria Anna Pertl

1751 Birth of Maria Anna Walburga ('Nannerl')

1756 Birth of Johann Chrysostom Wolfgang Amadeus Mozart, 27 January. Publication of Leopold Mozart's *Violin School*

1757 Leopold appointed court composer at Salzburg

1760 Wolfgang's first clavier lessons

1761 Leopold writes down Wolfgang's first compositions

1762 Wolfgang and Nannerl play at court in Munich and Vienna

1763 Wolfgang's early pieces published. Leopold appointed vice-*Kapellmeister* at Salzburg. First international tour, through the German courts to Paris

1764 From Paris to London. Wolfgang's first symphonies. Leopold seriously ill

1765 London to Holland

1766 Holland to France, Switzerland, Munich and back to Salzburg

1767 *Die Schuldigkeit des ersten Gebotes*; *Apollo et Hyacinthus*; first piano concertos. Visit to Vienna. Wolfgang and Nannerl both ill with smallpox

1768 *La Finta Semplice*; *Bastien und Bastienne*; first Mass

1769 First visit to Italy

1770 *Mitridate, Rè di Ponto* produced in Milan. Wolfgang elected member of the Accademia Filharmonico in Bologna

1771 Wolfgang appointed third *Konzertmeister* at Salzburg

1772 Hieronymus Colloredo enthroned as Prince Archbishop of Salzburg. *Lucio Silla*, second opera for Milan

1775 *La Finta Giardiniera* produced in Munich

1777 Wolfgang visits Munich and Mannheim, but fails to secure an appointment

1778 Falls in love with Aloysia Weber in Mannheim. Continues his journey to Paris. Death of his mother. Appears at Concert Spirituel. Rejects post of organist at Versailles

1779 Appointed court organist at Salzburg

1781 *Idomeneo* produced in Munich. Dismissed from his post in Salzburg. Freelance work in Vienna

1782 Marriage to Constanze Weber. *Die Entführung aus dem Serail* produced in Vienna

1783 Visits Salzburg with Constanze.

1784 Composing and concert-giving in Vienna. First surviving son, Karl Thomas, born

1785 Leopold Mozart visits Vienna. Six Haydn Quartets

1786 *Le Nozze di Figaro* produced in Vienna. Visit to Prague

1787 Death of Leopold. *Don Giovanni* produced in Prague. Appointed court composer to Emperor Joseph II

1788 *Don Giovanni* adapted and produced in Vienna

1789 Visit to Berlin, via Dresden and Leipzig. Prussian quartets commissioned

1790 *Così fan Tutte* produced in Vienna

1791 Franz Xaver Wolfgang, second son, born. *Die Zauberflöte* commissioned, composed and produced. The *Requiem* commissioned. *La Clemenza di Tito* written and produced for coronation of Leopold II in Prague. Death of Mozart, 5 December

A Note on Money

The nearest to a stable currency with an international rate of exchange in the late eighteenth century was the ducat, worth about nine shillings in the English money of the period.

In Germany and Austria at the time:

1 ducat $= 3\frac{1}{2} \begin{cases} \text{thalers} \\ \text{florins} \end{cases}$ 72 groschen

$\qquad\qquad 4\frac{1}{2}$ gulden   270 kreuzer

1 Friedrich d'or (basically Prussian) $= 7\frac{1}{2}$ gulden
1 Carolin (basically Bavarian) $= 9$ gulden
1 Louis d'or (basically French) $= 9$ gulden
1 souverain d'or (basically Austrian) $= 13\frac{1}{2}$ gulden.

The period of Mozart was that in which the 'Village Preacher' of Goldsmith's *The Deserted Village* was 'passing rich on forty pounds a year'.

Further Reading

Abert, H., *W. A. Mozart*. Leipzig, 1923, 1924.

Anderson, Emily, *The Letters of Mozart and his Family*, 3 vols. London, 1938.

Benn, C., *Mozart on the Stage*. London, 1946.

Bianciolli, Louis (ed.), *The Mozart Handbook*. New York, 1954.

Blom, Eric, *Mozart*. London, 1935.

Blom, Eric, *Mozart's Letters*. Harmondsworth, 1956.

Brophy, Brigid, *Mozart the Dramatist*. London, 1964.

Dent, E.J., *Mozart's Operas*. London, 1913, 1947.

Deutsch, Otto Erich, *Mozart: A Documentary Biography*, trans. E. Blom, P. Branscombe and J. Noble. London, 1965.

Dickinson, A. E. F., *Mozart's Last Three Symphonies*. London, 1927.

Dunhill, Thomas, *Mozart's String Quartets*. London, 1927.

Einstein, A., *Mozart: his Character, his Work*, trans. A. Mendel and N. Broder. London, 1946.

Girdlestone, C. M., *Mozart's Piano Concertos*. London, 1948.

Hill, Ralph (ed.), *The Symphony*. Harmondsworth, 1946.

Hill, Ralph (ed.), *The Concerto*. Harmondsworth, 1952.

Holmes, Edward, *The Life of Mozart*. London, 1845; E. Newman, London, 1912.

Hutchins, A., *A Companion to Mozart's Piano Concertos*. London, 1948.

Kenyon, Max, *Mozart in Salzburg*. London, 1952.

Kerman, Joseph, *Opera as Drama*. New York, 1952.

King, A. Hyatt, *Mozart in Retrospect*. London, 1956.

Landon, H. C. Robbins, *The Viennese Classical Style*. London, 1970.

Landon, H. C. Robbins and Mitchell, Donald (eds), *The Mozart Companion*. London, 1956.

Levarie, S., *Le Nozze di Figaro, a critical analysis*. Chicago, 1952.

Levey, Michael, *The Life and Death of Mozart*. London, 1971.

Saint-Foix, G. de, *The Symphonies of Mozart*, trans. Leslie Orrey. London, 1947.

Simpson, Robert (ed.), *The Symphony* (Vol. 1). Harmondsworth, 1966.

Sitwell, Sacheverell, *Mozart*. London, 1932.

Tovey, Donald F., *Essays in Musical Analysis* (Vols 1, 2, 3, 6). London, 1935–9.

Turner, W. J., *Mozart, the Man and his Works*. London, 1938.

Veinus, A., *The Concerto*. New York, 1948.

Wyzewa, T. and Saint-Foix, G. de, *W. A. Mozart, sa vie musicale et son oeuvre*, 5 vols. Paris, 1912–1946.

Index